Beyond
Prophetic

Chris Wren James

Beyond Prophetic

Onwards and Upwards Publishers
Berkeley House, 11 Nightingale Crescent, Leatherhead, Surrey, KT24 6PD.
www.onwardsandupwards.org

First published in the UK by Onwards and Upwards Publishers (2015).

Printed in the UK by 4edge Limited.

ISBN: 978-1-910197-46-2
Typeface: Sabon LT
Cover artwork: Rosie Moulton

The author has made every attempt to contact relevant copyright holders of quoted material, or has used material within Fair Use guidelines. The author will be glad to correct any possible omissions in future reprints of this publication.

Endorsements

"READ THIS BOOK! Many ministries are birthed through the prophetic word, and many survive and overcome through prophetic words. This book is essential teaching for the whole Body of Christ and I totally recommend it to everyone."

Elizabeth Burke
Regional Director of National Association of Healing Rooms
London, UK

"When a prophet speaks, their words drip with intentionality and import. When they teach, the lesson is magnified and anointed. Things you may have heard one hundred times you suddenly 'get'. When they pray, things shift. Just their presence brings change in the spirit realm. Prophets are concerned with the Kingdom because they love the King. Chris Wren James is such a one. A 'sent one'. One called to teach and train and release Kingdom truths. One sent to see people healed and released into the call of God on their lives. There are not many true apostles. Not many who see truly whom God has called you to be – who pray with you, walk the healing journey with you and ultimately train, activate and release you with true blessing – no control – no territorialism – just a heart full of the Father, truly blessed to see your success. Chris Wren James is such a one."

Debra Lee Page
Prophet, Worshipper, Song-writer

"I have known Chris Wren James for many years. She is a veteran Australian prophetic trainer and equipper with a deep passion to see a pure expression of New Testament prophetic ministry emerge throughout the church. Over the years I have had hours of encouraging conversations with Chris, and as I read her new book, 'Beyond Prophetic', I felt like I was in conversation with Chris once again.

Her style is relaxed and conversational but rich in profound insights that have been gleaned over a lifetime of cultivating prophetic discernment. Every paragraph is rich with prophetic wisdom on the theme of the call, the development and the role of the prophet in the local church.

Chris has walked through many seasons of the pilgrimage of the modern Pentecostal/Charismatic church, both here in Australia and also in her original homeland in England. She has walked through seasons of arid wilderness where the prophetic was totally misunderstood and rejected, and she has walked through seasons where the glory of the Lord has filled the temple and where entire congregations have been seized by an ecstatic prophetic anointing! Throughout the decades, Chris has faithfully called the people of God to lift up their vision and to contend for the day when all of God's people can prophesy.

And now, here we are on the verge of the greatest prophetic and apostolic move of God in human history as the glory of the Lord begins to cover the earth as the waters cover the sea. The wilderness years are fast becoming a distant memory as the saints are rising up to take the Land. In season and out of season, Chris has faithfully kept her eyes on the Promised Land.

During the wilderness years she has nurtured in her own heart the same qualities that Joshua and Caleb cultivated as they plodded through the wilderness dreaming of the day they would cross over into their true inheritance. Her book, 'Beyond Prophetic', is a good report of the Land that flows with milk and honey. There are mountains to be taken and giants to be slain but the Land that the

Lord has promised us is a good land and one worth fighting with all our strength in order to possess. Prophets have always kept their eyes on the Promised Land and have kept the pinnacles and mountain summits well within their sight. As they continue to focus on the future destiny of the people of God they are sharpened in their capacity to describe and articulate the glory of our inheritance.

This book, packed with rich prophetic insights, is a roadmap for emerging prophetic ministers to glean from a veteran equipper who has learned a thousand valuable lessons and has gathered these lessons into a readable assembly of sections and chapters that are well worth the time taken to read. One of the things I like the most about Chris's conversational writing style is the down-to-earth, matter-of-fact way that she expresses her heart. She loves people, and behind the scenes she is content to just keep on pouring herself into many people who have benefitted from her straightforward style in counselling and prayer ministry.

I heartily recommend Chris as a proven prophetic minister with a wonderful prophetic gift. Both Chris and her husband, Steve, are faithful members of the spiritual community that my wife and I lead. On countless occasions we have been the beneficiaries of her prophetic words and her encouragement, and I know of dozens of people both in our church and our region who have received significant prophetic words from Chris over the years. It brings a broad smile to my face to keep meeting new people from all over our region who have received prophetic words from Chris over the past few decades. Our community is indeed much the richer for having Chris investing herself and her gift, both publicly and behind the scenes. I hope you enjoy reading what she has written and that you will garner countless insights for your own development in the prophetic ministry."

Phil Mason
Apostle and Spiritual Director, New Earth Tribe, Australia

"Christine is a seasoned prophet and an original wild woman of God. She has given her life for the establishment of a true prophetic river flowing in many nations. I know hundreds who have been impacted by her gifting and life, both in personal prophecy and personal prayer ministry. I have known Christine for many years and watched with joy as her prophetic gift has released life through power and deliverance. She is a perfect blend of prophet and deliverer!

I am super excited to endorse this book, as it comes from years of experience and ploughing in the fields that at the beginning were hard and indifferent to the prophetic ministry. Chris has been responsible for helping to shift that culture here in Australia and abroad in England, where she worked for many years. She is a mother of what I would call the 'true prophets' in our nation; those who are devoted to intimacy, the healing of the heart, the warmth and love of the local church and the development of the apostolic paradigm. I have no reserve at all in endorsing her life, her work, or her ministry.

Chris is a true lover of God, a woman who fights her battles valiantly and walks in supernatural grace.

Apart from all that, she likes a good coffee and lots of laughter – and that makes her one of my dear friends. I highly recommend this new book to you. It is a very thorough work on the prophetic and has much insight into developing your gifting. You will love it!"

Maria Mason
Prophet, Musician/Worshipper
Co-director, New Earth Tribe, Byron Bay, Australia.

Preface

This book has been evolving in my heart for some time now, waiting for the "now" time, the "kairos" moment in God, to publish. The original teaching manual has been taught over many years in many places including Australia, South Africa, England, France and Canada, allowing many to discover their particular spiritual gifting, and begin to use it for the glory of God. I have now re-written and added largely to the original.

Every gift carries its own treasure and its own responsibility. My passion is to enable people everywhere to find the treasure within, the Pearl of Great Price – Jesus. There are two rails in my calling as a prophet-teacher and I take this responsibility very seriously. I take great joy in equipping people who are interested in the areas of the prophetic by teaching prophetic schools. I also have a desire to see the church healed, restored, alert and fully immersed in life. My other rail is in teaching restoration healing schools and training others in this important area.

It is vital that we demonstrate Jesus in all His amazing aspects in the best possible way, particularly in prophetic ministry. Revelation 19:10 says that *"the substance (essence) of the truth revealed by Jesus is the spirit of all prophecy"* (AMP). We need to portray Him in truth.

Finally, prophets and prophetic ministry are entering a time of greater integrity and credibility in the church, particularly in the areas of ethics and protocol. I pray that this book will answer some questions and bless you beyond your wildest dreams.

Christine Wren James
Director, Life Streams International
www.lifestreamsinternational.net
info@lifestreamsinternational.net

Acknowledgements

"Thanks be to God for His indescribable gift."
(2 Corinthians 9:15, NIV)

Thanks be to God, my *real* Father. You continually demonstrate infinite loving patience to me, in spite of all my failings. You float my boat. Words fail me, but I love you forever.

Thanks to my very real family, down to the last grandchild. You keep me grounded but always looking forward. I love you because we all believe in each other hugely, and believe the best. You are *all* my favourites.

Thanks my real friends in lands everywhere. You know who you are. You've pushed me along the stream and never judged me. You've told me the truth in love, when I least wanted it but most needed it. Thank you. Don't stop.

Thank you, Steve, my patiently loving, ever-serving hubbie – who ignores my "nitchiness" and leaves me to write. You are the rock to my kite. You are my hero, Superman.

Thanks, Maria and Phil, prophet/apostle combo and Spiritual Directors of New Earth Tribe, the church we have loved to serve. You demonstrate honour to everyone you know. I have learnt a new dimension.

Thanks, Rosie M, amazing artist/designer; favour on you big time.

Contents

Definition: Prophet

"Prophet, pro'fit n. a spokesman of deity; one who pro-
claims a divine message: an inspired teacher, preacher or
poet; the spokesman of a group, movement or doctrine;
a minister of the second order of the Catholic Apostolic
church; a foreteller, whether claiming to be inspired or
not..."

Chambers Twentieth Century Dictionary

CHAPTER ONE

Are We Nearly There, Dad?

The million dollar question we are all asking ourselves is, "Where are we now?"

I believe that the next level, the next place, we find ourselves in, is bringing us out of all we have relied on – to throw us totally on God. Jesus says in Matthew 16:18, *"...and on this rock I will build my church and the gates of hell shall not overcome it."* (NIV) The church is now being built through the men and women who are rising up in the calling that God is releasing. The church has always been built by faithful men and women of God who knew what they were called to do and did it. Jesus gives us many keys to the Kingdom but the house is His to build.

God is sharpening the sword, the cutting edge of His Word, cutting through religious trivia, status symbols and the way we have always done things. His laser light is exposing the one place where Satan has access – what we hide in the dark. He is exposing the extent to which we are enslaved to the wisdom of the age and the spirit of the age. We are in a time *"...for judgement to begin with the household of God..."* (1 Peter 4:17, AMP), and it can look like chaos for a while before order comes.

Have you ever been present at the birth of a baby in the delivery room? It's chaotic, loud and messy. All of it is necessary for what is new in God to be birthed, nurtured and matured.

In Proverbs 24:3,4 we learn that knowledge fills the house but wisdom builds it. Knowledge is something we acquire but wisdom can come from the mind of God as a gift. We need to pray for the wisdom and revelation of the knowledge of God.

If the pastor, evangelist, or teacher anointing was going to bring the church into maturity it would have done so by now, but it has not. It will take the apostle/prophet dynamic, now being released into the body of Christ globally, to do this in spite of many impediments. This next equipping will bring many challenges and many opportunities to be offended. The arm of the church has been withered to a degree but is now reaching out with the new life of the prophetic/apostolic injected into its blood stream.

The Wife of God is Not De-facto (or Common Law)

The Father heart of God is one of total, 100% commitment. He is not like us, thank God. In fact, thank God for God. He never has a bad day or a bad minute and He is always the same – fabulously full and overflowing with benevolent love. He is our Father, and we are all His favourites.

He is radical and outside the box we have tried to put Him in for a sense of our own safety and control. Respectability and conformity are not fruits of the Holy Spirit and can often tend to wrap us up in religious "hoo-ha". Respect and dignity offered through love are another thing entirely. The old ways of "doing church", that now seem boring and predictable, are dying a slow death in wilderness camps everywhere.

There are thousands of un-churched Christians out there with better things to do on a Sunday than look at the back of someone's head and believe that they are having intimate fellowship just because someone says to greet someone you don't know. I am coming to believe that the type of "fellowship" that the Lord has in mind for us is based on intimate sharing, mutual transparency and a deeper level of friendship than we have dared imagine. It's about facing our fears of rejection and allowing religious facades to drop off.

The Lord of glory says, "Welcome to the show!" God is showing His hand and laying down His cards for all to see. He is showing us off to the world, as a demonstration of love. He is showing His hands and His feet – in fact, His body – in ways we never dreamed possible. He is being seen and heard in a different way with a different sound. He is appearing in places and in people that may have once offended our sensibilities – all outside the church walls, no less! This is the shape of things to come now emerging. We've never been this way before, thankfully. There is no particular blueprint or map for it, just trust and the peace that comes from knowing that this is the Holy Spirit, which lets *the peace of Christ rule in [our] hearts"* (Colossians 3:15, NIV). The Amplified version says, *"...let the peace ... from Christ ... (act as an umpire)..."* I won't blow the whistle on that.

The church is the bride He has chosen for His Son Jesus and she is now being prepared for that wedding by many attendants and bridesmaids. This means all of the five-fold ministers who equip and prepare and are in another paradigm – consultant ministries to the body.

Sometimes the church can have a de-facto heart. In a de-facto relationship neither partner wants to commit by covenant or promise. The back door remains open, or at least ajar, and in particular the "wife" does not want to give up her name to take on another's, to lose her identity. In a postmodern society this is all par for the course and often denotes lack of trust from earlier wounding. Understandably.

If Jesus had a real wife she would not be selfish, unkind or inhospitable. Jesus does not dismember Himself. She would not have an adulterous heart either. God already divorced His wife for that once (Jeremiah 3:8).

God longs for us as His bride, His church with a passion, and wants us to love Him and Him alone with an undivided heart.

How Did We Get To Be Here?

For the first five-hundred years the church flourished and moved in great anointing, great authority and excellent structure.

THE JERUSALEM CHURCH:

The very first church was birthed on the day of Pentecost, as the disciples and others were gathered together in one place. Suddenly there came a sound from heaven. This sound was like that of *"a violent tempest blast"* (Acts 2:2, AMP). Tongues of fire appeared on them and they began to *"speak in other ... languages ... [with] clear and loud expression"*. About three-thousand people received Christ on that day. This birthed the first church. It was messy, loud, and powerful with a raw sound of reality.

This church came under great persecution from the day that Stephen was stoned to death, with Paul (called Saul, before his conversion) commending and consenting to his death. The Jerusalem church was then scattered and inadvertently became a "sending" church through the scattering of the believers. This church was never able to break free of Judaism due to the number of Jews who attended.

THE ANTIOCH CHURCH:

The next church to be established was at Antioch and consisted of a mixture of Jews and Gentiles. Great revival broke out in Antioch as the Word was preached with power. Barnabas arrived in Antioch from the church at Jerusalem, being *"a good man, full of the Holy spirit and faith"* (Acts 11:24, NIV), and a huge amount of people were added to the church. Barnabas then went off to find Saul and brought him back to Antioch, where they met with the church and taught them extensively for twelve months.

It was in Antioch that the believers were first called "Christians". Prophets also came down from Jerusalem to Antioch. They prophesied of the famine to come, thus bringing a helpful warning and the church was able to prepare for it. There was a lot of grace on the Antioch church (Acts 11:23).

This church became a "sending" apostolic church. The life came from the people and they were generous givers. It replaced the Jerusalem church in time. Their problem was that arguments arose over Jewish law and circumcision (Galatians 2:13) and Paul ultimately regarded that church as unsuitable.

THE EPHESIAN CHURCH:

The church was eventually built to the model found in Ephesians 2:19b-21 (NIV): *"...you are ... built upon the foundation of the apostles and prophets with Christ Jesus himself the chief cornerstone. In him the whole building is joined together [harmoniously] and rises to become a holy temple... "*

It was here that Paul clearly set out the walk of the church, its guidelines and parameters. In Acts 19, we find Paul has arrived in Ephesus and found about twelve disciples, who have been baptized into *"John's baptism"* (NIV), which included repentance. Paul lays hands on them and they become filled with the Holy Spirit and begin to prophesy.

For the following two years we find that Paul holds meetings every day from 10am until 3pm, in the lecture room of Tyrannus. Those present included these twelve disciples.

Acts 19:10 states that *"[all] of Asia heard the word of the Lord"* (NIV). Miracles begin to happen and prayer cloths were laid on the sick and the demonized, and God's power and anointing was released through Paul and his disciples.

Thousands of pounds sterling worth of books on magic arts and sorcery were burnt in a big bonfire and *"the Word of the Lord ... grew ... prevailing mightily"* (Acts 19:20, AMP). Many times the Word being preached and prophesied caused a riot needing crowd control.

The Ephesian church had become the major apostolic church in the known world. It was here that Paul received two great revelations:

1. That the Gentiles were able to obtain salvation.
2. That the church was in fact the body of Christ.

The first revelation that was revealed to the apostles and the prophets was that the Gentiles are now to be fellow heirs with the Jews, joint partakers in the same divine promise through the glad tidings of the Gospel (Ephesians 3:5-6). *"[This mystery] was never disclosed to human beings in past generations as it has now been revealed to His holy apostles (conecrated messengers) and prophets by the [Holy] Spirit."* (verse 9, AMP).

The second revelation is found in 1 Corinthians 12:27 where we read, *"Now you [collectively] are Christ's body and [individually] you are members of it, each part ... distinct."* (AMP) Paul had the revelation of the church ideally being *"one body, with one Spirit ... one God and father of all, who is over all and through all and in all."* (Ephesians 4:4, AMP). In fact, the actual and original meaning of the word "catholic" comes from the Greek "katholikos" and means "universal". Its original intention was to be all embracing of Christian believers everywhere, totally liberal – the opposite to exclusivity.

In the book of Revelation in chapter 2, the church at Ephesus was highly commended for its industriousness and patient endurance but was upbraided for abandoning its first love.

The eldership leadership was functional, but only as a plurality.

> It was he who gave some to be apostles, some to be prophets, some to be evangelists, and some to be pastors and teachers.
>
> *Ephesians 4:11 (NIV)*

By 500AD the church was backslidden, and the powerful five-fold ministry application which had been the very foundation of the Christian church had diminished and almost disappeared entirely. It was replaced by the hierarchy of Pope, Cardinal, Archbishop, Bishop and Priest. For over 1800 years the church has not had altogether biblical foundations, generally speaking, and a lot of the original power and anointing for miracles and healing has been lost along the way. However, what was instituted first (i.e. the office of apostle and secondly prophets) is now being re-instituted at the end of the age as God aligns His church into what she was originally intended to be.

Ephesians 2:19b-20 clearly states: *"...you are ... built upon the foundation of the apostles and prophets, with Christ Jesus himself as the chief cornerstone."* (NIV) What was actually first is now being instituted last.

In 1517 Martin Luther declared that *"the just shall live by faith"* (Hebrews 10:38, AMP). Martin Luther is referred to as a prophet by some historians, and was persecuted by the existing church leaders who were quick to excommunicate him and label him a heretic. He created a furore, a revolution amongst church leaders. It overthrew existing church doctrine and structure, as was needed at the time.

A Short History of the Five-Fold Ministry

The five-fold ministry, which will be referred to many times in this book, refers to the gift and function of apostles, prophets, teachers, evangelists and pastors. *"It was he who gave some to be apostles, some to be prophets, some to be evangelists, and some to be pastors and teachers."* (Ephesians 4:11, NIV). Each of these ministry gifts are like the five fingers on the hand of God, moving the body of Christ.

In 1 Corinthians 12:28 (AMP), in describing how parts of the church operate, Paul says, *"So God has appointed some in the church [for His own use]: first apostles ... second prophets ... third teachers ... then wonder-workers; then those with ability to heal the sick; helpers; administrators; [speakers in] different (unknown) tongues."* The use of the word "some" obviously denotes that there will be some called to this office but not all. There is in effect no mention of pastors or evangelists in this passage.

The five-fold is literally the gift and extension of Jesus Himself to the church. Its main function is to *"equip his people for works of service, so that the body of Christ may be built up"* (Ephesians 4:12, NIV). As we have not yet attained the *"oneness in the faith and in*

17

the comprehension of the [full and accurate] knowledge of the Son of God, that [we might arrive] at really mature manhood {of the faith}" (Ephesians 4:13, AMP) we can safely assume that the equipping by the five-fold must still continue.

The church needs to be built on the foundation of the prophets and apostles (Ephesians 2:20). Up to now the church has been equipped by the three-fold (i.e. pastors, teachers and evangelists), and it has become a three-fold cord that is not easy to untie to include the other two. We need the totality of the fullness of Christ, not just a few parts. As helpful and useful as the gifts of pastors, teachers and evangelists are, it will not be sufficient to usher the Body of Christ into the age we are entering into, because it is only three of the five-fold ministries.

Each place of enlargement is like entering through the narrow gate, or the eye of the needle, and is entered into through much stress. When God threads us through that eye, He knows exactly when and where to place us in the tapestry of our lives. Like a birthing, the birth canal is constricting and painful, and by stage three of labour we just want to get the baby out *now!* Once the baby is placed in our arms we forget the pain and enter into joy. There are many birthings in unusual places just now. Some are quiet and hidden and God does not reveal the baby until the right moment. For some it is a time of patience and trust.

At every level we go into we need to die to any reputation we might have acquired in the one before.

Yes, it's painful, and yes, it is an identity with the sufferings of Christ who was betrayed by friends, His character assassinated; He went through death and out the other side into glory. It's important to learn how to die quietly and with as much dignity as we can muster. Dying to our reputation teaches us, too, that we don't have to be right all the time and we can't control everybody. All ultimately very helpful.

God's Generals

Approximately every hundred years God has released His generals to impart certain truths to the church. From about 1950 onward, it seems that certain truths have been released to the church about every ten years up to the present day. These are in fact apostles of present day truth, found in the word of God. Today's apostles are ushering in an age of unity that carries diversity, not conformity or a divisive spirit. Some churches are meant to split for greater growth, however, or simply close and die for a resurrection in a new form. When true unity is present we are *"no longer ... tossed ... to and fro"* (Ephesians 4:14, AMP). A good prophet/apostle dynamic in a church will cause the wanderers to settle and bring a stability that people are attracted to and feel safe in.

The three main things that block a new move of God are fear, unbelief, and unaddressed wounds. The restoration healing movement of the last twenty years has been incredibly beneficial in exposing and healing deep wounding in the church, allowing people to be honest about their lives, their emotions and their brokenness. It is so important to minister from the brokenness that leads to an understanding of God's grace and humility, rather than ministering from the anger and depression that come from our wounds.

Decades of Release

God moved mightily through the Wesley brothers in England, and revival came. Many wonderful hymns were written and enjoyed in a church environment. The Methodist church was founded; however it is no longer the cutting edge.

John Calvin brought new truths to the church – the Baptist church was formed, with an emphasis on total immersion at baptism.

William Booth and family began to minister to the poor and needy. It is still their main mandate. Thousands of people were brought to a knowledge of Jesus. A doctrine of soup, soap and salvation was birthed. Christian lyrics were put to the music of the day and played in the streets. Many churches were outraged at such an overt display. A radical departure emerged from the solemnity of existing church music, which had been only for the select few.

Each wave of revelation has brought a new truth, but each has camped at the revelation and not moved on. When a movement becomes a monument it can become religion and idolatry. It can become the "golden calf" set in the concrete of the day.

In 1900 a great move of God was ushered in at a supernatural outpouring of the Holy Spirit in Azusa Street, USA, and other localities simultaneously. Revival broke out and God restored the truth of the baptism of Holy Spirit with speaking in tongues.

When a church is revived it is simply about returning to the original intention of that church. We can and often do become as religious and traditional as any other denomination. Every denomination has wanted to "box" and own God. Most of us may perhaps have been drawn to become Pharisees in Jesus' day, as they had good family values and they loved the Word of God. But they were bound in the traditions of men, which is always a trap and a deterrent to moving on in the Spirit of God.

The Five-Fold Restoration to the Church

> He gave some as apostles, some as prophets, and some as evangelists and some as pastors and teachers for the equipping of the saints for the work of service, to the building up of the body of Christ. Until we all attain to the unity of the faith and to the knowledge of the Son of God and become mature attaining to the whole measure of the fullness of Christ.
>
> *Ephesians 4:11-13 (NASB)*

The word "equip" literally means, "prepare, train, make fully qualified for service, to set a bone in place". If you have ever put your back out and needed a chiropractor to "put it back in", you will know what it is to be unable to stand straight or walk until the problem is rectified. Until the believers in a church are equipped, there will be little maturity and people remain needy, dependant and immature.

Jesus Himself is all five giftings, and I believe that although each five-fold minister may move in one or two of these offices at some time, only Jesus contains the whole five at any one time in their fullness. We are called as ministers of grace, of reconciliation, of love, and of the covenant of God but we are not *all* called to be five-fold ministers, only "some".

The gift *is* the men and women themselves who are five-fold ministers, given by God to the church for the equipping of the church, until the church has reached the fullness and maturity and stature of the Lord Jesus Christ. We understand that we are not yet in that place of maturity or unity, therefore the "equipping of the saints" shall be continued.

Decades of Restoration

In the 1950s we saw the restoration of the five-fold gift of evangelist to the church fairly globally (e.g. Oral Roberts, Billy Graham, Kathryn Kuhlman, and many others).

Men and women travelled all over the world as evangelists. Thousands were convicted of their sins and brought to salvation as another truth was restored to the church. What was the music of the day? Hymns based on the Word of God, mainly solemn and serious. Many still remember the hymn "Just as I Am" as Billy Graham's calling card which brought hundreds of people from their seats in grandstands across the world rushing to Jesus and the call for salvation.

In the 1960s we saw the restoration of the five-fold gift of pastor as head of the church. We experienced the charismatic renewal and what was called the release of the "Jesus people". There was an emphasis on the truth of being "born again" restored into church. What did we sing? We began to sing scripture, folk/gospel. Christian musicals began to emerge, and the dawn of the hippie movement began to be birthed in the world. It was a radical change both secularly and in the church.

Feminism began powerfully and women began to emerge with an identity they had never been allowed to have. Australia and America fought in the Vietnam War. There was much political and social change. I was changed radically from the strong feminist views of the early 70s, having earlier embraced a more or less "hippie" approach to life of "if it feels good, do it". My encounter with Jesus was powerful and life-changing, and I have never ceased being grateful for the life He has given me.

In the 1970s we saw the restoration of the five-fold gift of teacher right across the church. Cassette tapes and cassette players began to abound. There was a strong emphasis on the teaching on faith as the faith movement emerged. Prosperity teaching, faith confession and victorious living were preached as the truth of faith was restored to the church. What did we sing? More Scripture in song, songs about the church being a family, more musicals, as well as more folk/gospel songs.

We saw the release of Christian pop stars as some Christian music actually touched secular space. Records and cassettes of Christian music were released on to the market. The marketing end of the Gospel began to be big business.

The 1980s saw the beginning of the prophetic movement globally, and the restoration of the prophet as a five-fold gift to the church, and the truth of prophecy began to be brought to the church. Quietly and unobtrusively, companies of prophets came together; there was activation of the gifts, warfare, intercession and prophets being sent to nations.

The prophetic ministry still continues to grow in integrity and credibility so as to be received back into the general ministry of the church. As this is accomplished and settles I believe there will come again a great sending of missionary apostles, particularly to poorer nations, to undergird and build strong foundations in the churches there.

Also in the 1980s, the concept of the truth of emotional healing and deliverance began to be seen and experienced, and the restoration healing movement began. What did we sing? Songs of war and songs of worship. Christian rock bands began to emerge and the boat began to be rocked in the church, both in music and ministry.

The 1990s signalled the restoration of the apostle and the apostolic movement. There will be more written about this in later chapters. We began to see signs and wonders, healings and miracles and a greater sending out of the apostolic evangelist.

The government is being restored to the church based on the Kingdom rather than hierarchy. This is currently turning established hierarchical structures upside down – and is meant to. There is no Biblical basis for a denomination, only the local church, whether that be in a public place or a house setting.

What did we sing? We began to sing the song of the Lord, the song of the Lamb, releasing the sounds from heaven, with angelic accompaniment at times.

There is now a changing of the old guard for the new. God is always doing something new and wonderful. His character never changes but He carries change.

There are many more Christians outside of hierarchical churches now than in. God has always given a person a revelation and anointed it to build a local body of believers. Unity is more about having enough love and maturity to embrace diversity than merely conforming and becoming a clone. It is built on relationships and never merely function. The Trinity is relational – each relates to the others. As we spend time as a group, a mob, a church, a body, eating together, listening and genuinely loving and being vulnerable to one another instead of simply looking at the back of heads once a week on a Sunday, God will build His church in a most amazing and transforming way.

The Mighty Hand of God

To simplify this teaching: each one of the five-fold ministries can be depicted as the Finger of God on the Hand of God.

THE THUMB – THE APOSTLE:

Every finger relates to the thumb, representative of the apostle. This office is marked with authority, humility, suffering and patience. It is the governmental office in the body of Christ which essentially sorts out, fixes up, addresses the issues and re-defines the borders in churches and nations. Apostolic anointing is big. It is marked by authority and fearlessness. The fleshly flipside is control and bullying, selfish ambition and territorialism.

> So for the sake of Christ, I am well pleased and take pleasure in infirmities, insults, hardships, persecutions, perplexities and distresses; for when I am weak [in human strength], then am I [truly] strong (able, powerful in divine strength).
>
> *2 Corinthians 12:10 (AMP)*
>
> Indeed, the signs that indicate a [genuine] apostle were performed among you fully and most patiently in miracles and wonders and mighty works.
>
> *2 Corinthians 12:12 (AMP)*

Apostolic anointing crushes religious systems and is like a "Samson anointing" – to bring down the Babylonian systems of the world and establish God's government and God's Kingdom, rather than hierarchical status.

"The government will be on his shoulders" (Isaiah 9:6, NIV) is the function of the apostle. Our first government is self-government, bringing our soul under the dominion of the spirit. Apostolic government is Kingdom-based government.

The motion of coming from the opposite direction gives power to the hand. The thumb is not in opposition to the other fingers but the four fingers need the thumb to function adequately.

Apostles will move in miracles and in healing, faith, wisdom, discerning of spirits and prophecy – all with the heart of the father, and in humility.

The basic root meaning of the word apostle is, "one sent as a representative of another," like an ambassador of the king with the power and authority coming from the one who sent him. His continuing ministry is based on how successfully he conveys the heart and message of the king.

THE POINTING FINGER – THE PROPHET:

This finger points, dissects, announces, sniffs out the enemies to the prophet, which are fear, manipulation, control and religiosity – many facets that are in the Jezebel Power. Jezebel is the archenemy of the prophet.

Prophets preach repentance! They love to change things in the spirit realm, ceaselessly toiling, are microscopic, high sensory, super-sensitive, and easily rejected. They need to get alone with God constantly and love the solitude of the mountain.

When prophets have finished ministering, they generally like to go home immediately it is over and avoid the "chit-chat", otherwise known as "meaningful fellowship" that others who are more pastoral love. They get "peopled-out" quickly.

They always love to, and are always able to, prophesy. They carry an exposing anointing which peels off facades and masks, lays things bare to the bones with an almost tangible anointing. Prophets often cry when others laugh and vice-versa. What can look like a small deal to others is a big deal to a prophet, because of the gift of seeing and knowing. There is often the fear of the Lord in not discharging all they have been sent to do.

The heart of the prophet is the heart of God.

> Surely the Sovereign LORD does nothing without revealing his
> plan to his servants the prophets.
>
> *Amos 3:7 (NIV)*

God is currently releasing His prophets and prophetic companies of people across the world. This is part of the fulfilment of the scripture:

> Behold, I will send you Elijah the prophet before the coming of the great and dreadful day of the LORD:
> And he shall turn the heart of the fathers to the children, and the heart of the children to their fathers...
>
> *Malachi 4:5-6a (KJV)*

The promise of the return of Elijah was initially fulfilled in John the Baptist – *"And if you are willing to receive and accept it, John himself is Elijah who was to come [before the Kingdom]"* (Matthew 11:14, AMP) – and also in the prophesy from the angel of the Lord to John's father Zachariah in Luke 1:17, that John *"...will [himself] go before Him in the spirit and power of Elijah..."* (AMP). However, the actual implication of the spirit of Elijah is the prophetic emphasis of the Holy Spirit releasing the voice of God prophetically across the world through His prophets and prophetic people everywhere.

Prophets represent the five senses of the body of Christ and the trumpet of God blasting through every generation. Sometimes trumpets are loud and irritating and disturb the status quo, but they are representative of announcing, waking people up and signalling a season.

> Prophets often have major assaults and assignments against them from Satan from birth and even before birth to prevent them moving into their calling, which will always expose darkness and release light. Many prophets have struggled with immense fear, unusual amounts of abuse, physical, emotional and spiritual, in an effort to keep them wounded and shut down and therefore non-functional. Many modern day prophets have stories of survival, as I do too.

Most prophets (certainly those who are healed), love to see the treasure in the earthen vessel, the gold in the dirt, and the potential in people. I believe it is essential that prophets work towards their own recovery and healing so that the purity of the words from God come through the cleanest vehicle possible.

Some people avoid prophets, believing that prophets can "see their whole life" in glorious Technicolor. Of course the truth is that prophets who know that they are sent by God to encourage and love bring out the ultimate best in every person through their gifting, and draw out, by prophesying, that which God has planted and planned for every person. We all have a longing to know who we are, and I believe prophets play a major role in expressing through prophecy and, through the love of God, exactly what each person is called to be.

The main functions of the prophet are:

1. To teach people to hear from God themselves.
   This is the most important function of a prophet.
2. To set people into their calling by the prophetic word.
   A classic example is, *"See I have this day appointed you to the oversight of the nations and of the Kingdoms – to root out, to pull down, to destroy and to overthrow, to build and to plant."* (Jeremiah 1:10, AMP).
3. To settle the wanderers.
   People are generally tired of control and religiosity, and because prophets are passionately against both of these, people can begin to feel safe amongst prophets of God and finally feel at home.
4. To work beside the other four of five-fold (if the other four will allow it, of course).
   Together they can then equip the church.
5. To search for and rescue the wounded and disqualified, and bring them to a safe resting place to recover and find strength for the battle again.

Many prophets operate in the Healing Movement, having recovered their own wholeness first. In my own prophetic ministry this is the other "rail" on the track, and one of my passions is to see captive people released and delivered, getting back into the race again.

6. <u>To provide direction for ministries and people.</u>
7. <u>To bring clear vision to the church.</u>
   If there are no prophets, no eyes and no vision, the church will stumble in half-light.
8. <u>To bring correction, if mature and seasoned.</u>
   However, most prophets hate bringing correction because of their own sensitivities.
9. <u>To impart spiritual gifts.</u>
   Paul explains this by saying, *"For I am yearning to see you, that I may impart and share with you some spiritual gift to strengthen and establish you"* (Romans 1:11, AMP). We give what has been freely bestowed on us. This enables the church to move into all she has been called to do with each part functioning as it ought.
10. <u>To anoint ministries and release people into their calling,</u> particularly into five-fold ministry.
    God always speaks to the potential in a person, and not always to the "now" we might be trapped in, or the past where we have failed. Gideon, a depressed and frightened man, hiding in a winepress, is a classic case of God calling out who he was meant to be. We can tend to be drawn to the potential in us called out by a prophet and rise to that. This is the *"<u>that</u> for which Christ … has laid hold of me"* (AMP, emphasis added) directive from Paul in Philippians 3:12.
11. <u>To learn to walk through rejection.</u>
    It is often not personal and can simply be the rejection of all that the office brings that is challenging, disruptive and offensive to the religious sensibilities that exist everywhere.

12. To check their own attitudes and hearts to ensure that people are meeting a bigger percentage of Christ than the person who brings Him into the mix.

THE THIRD FINGER – THE EVANGELIST:

The evangelist is represented by the finger in the middle of lots of activity. It has a "drawing" anointing of all people. The evangelist draws big crowds, and is often a showman, a salesman, a great communicator and entertainer. They are often loud and demonstrative, make people laugh, and can be clowns, but are deadly serious about their call to evangelism. They often go in first to take the word of salvation.

Many evangelists have had a life-changing conversion, even near-death experiences or actual death experiences with visions of heaven and hell included. They are obsessed with getting everyone saved because this is their call. They attract attention and love the challenge of the unchurched crowd, secular space, poorer nations and other cultures such as the New Age culture, to introduce Christ. An evangelists often has a strong healing anointing. They are no good as a pastor, as it is not their calling at all; besides, they are called to come and go.

These people do not usually have a shepherd's heart; rather they are fishers of men, who catch fish, big and small, in the net but bring them to others to cut off the heads and rip open the guts. When a local church is operating with all five of the five-fold ministry gifts functioning as they ought, evangelists are free to go and rescue the perishing, snatch them from the fire and bring them to a safe place for teaching and restoration.

THE RING FINGER – THE PASTOR:

The pastor is married to the church and has the heart of the Shepherd Jesus.

Pastors are in for the long haul. They love the sheep, love to rescue, comfort, enfold, and keep them all safe. Often pastors keep prophets away to safeguard the sheep and avoid chaos. Prophets may be seen as disruptive and uncaring by the pastor.

The most difficult dynamic today is probably that of pastor and prophet working together in some sort of unified function. Again, relationship is crucial to this working effectively. Pastors can be threatened by prophetic anointing, because it can be laser-sharp and focused, throwing off the comfort of layers of pastoral leadership. It can reveal the true calling and identity of many of the people who felt guilty about who they knew they were really, deep down, because it might change the status quo in the church.

The pastoral anointing comforts, consoles, counsels, visits and counts all the sheep to ensure none is missing. Like Moses, he listens to the bleating of the sheep. Moses died when he was still fit and able, in order to make way for Joshua, who was a representative of apostolic authority. It takes an apostolic warrior anointing to take people out of wilderness times and into the Promised Land.

The biggest block to the "new thing" is to hang on to the old. Those in the old will very often persecute those who embrace the new, and human nature decrees we will criticize, even mock, what we do not understand. When a church is moving into new territory, those who want to stay behind need to be left behind or they can seriously impede the progress of the whole.

The Promised Land was certainly about more than milk and honey and grapes; it was also about giants, demon kings and fortified cities. Warfare will always be about strategy and alertness, spoils and victories to be won. The pastor is an essential five-fold gift to the body but if there is going to be a clash at all in the five-fold gifts it will usually be between the pastor and the prophet

THE FIFTH FINGER – THE TEACHER:

Today's teacher brings revelation knowledge to the church, particularly if he/she has a prophetic edge. They can bring change, challenge the status quo, and bring understanding and knowledge. When asked to preach they will usually teach, and will use various resources including whiteboards, and the latest technology such as PowerPoint etc. They always have the right book, podcast or DVD for you. They have all versions of the Bible on the shelf (and on their phones).

Teachers may have years of treasure locked inside them and are a vital gift for new Christians to glean from. They can operate with a gift of the word of wisdom and are usually extremely "Word based" and well read. They are a vital ministry to church progressing in this hour.

Prophets and teachers abounded in the early church years and are essential in conveying doctrine and truth.

The Pastor / Prophet Clash

The two most crucial areas needed to establish a good protocol bridge today are prophets and pastors as well as apostles and prophets. Teachers usually have a good overlap with pastors and they tend to work well as a five-fold gift together.

2 Chronicles 20:20 says, *"...Believe in the Lord your God and you shall be established; believe and remain steadfast to His prophets and you shall prosper."* (AMP)

Pastoring a prophet is probably a learned skill and very individualized. Many prophets have been deeply wounded in churches through misunderstanding on all sides and have to learn to trust again. Like everyone, the healing of earlier wounding is vital, or a prophet will minister from that base and can hurt a lot of people. Prophets simply want to feel safe and not be abused by leadership. They need to be nurtured both personally and in their gifting. I believe it is vital for prophets to have a deep understanding of the Word of God, and know too that the Word and the Spirit must agree.

Some prophets are over-zealous and even pushy, but if you have been in prophetic ministry for over ten years you will have bruises and wounding but hopefully wisdom – even in hindsight.

Prophets are keenly aware of being answerable to God. Pastors are aware of their own accountability too but they also have to pastor the people, and see the elders on Monday morning. There are two main fears of prophets and pastors. The prophet fears that they might not discharge all that has been required by God; the pastor fears that the church will get too excited and move into hype.

If only ONE of the five-fold gifting is involved in the church:

- <u>Pastor only</u>: There will be people with deep relationships but perhaps not enough vision.
- <u>Apostle only</u>: Apostles are called to go frequently and plant and establish in other places and regions; he/she will be away a lot, and unless the base church is set up adequately with other five-fold ministers in place, there will be chaos.
- <u>Evangelist only</u>: This church will tend to be very salvation-focused only, full of new converts and immaturity. The evangelist is called to come and go and be with the unchurched a lot. If an evangelist is running the church, it might be a church a mile-wide and an inch deep.
- <u>Teacher only</u>: There will be lots of teaching, naturally, but the church will become a lecture hall.
- <u>Prophet only</u>: There will be lots of revelation and experiences and worship but often not enough of the basic Word taught. Most prophetic churches are small and full of wounded, battle-weary warriors.

Prophets are ostensibly encouragers who qualify the disqualified and call people into their true identity in God. God is on the move, as usual, showing us how to move in these exciting days we are in, with a minimum of madness and a maximum of love.

to be an apostle," yet he conducted evangelistic campaigns, pastored churches in several places, taught at length and was an itinerant minister. Nevertheless his main calling was as an apostle.

We do not choose the call – the call chooses us. We are usually "seen to be doing" the thing that possesses us long before anyone actually acknowledges that we are. Our destiny in God is simply, *"that for which Christ Jesus ... has laid hold of me and made me His own"* (Philippians 3:12b, AMP, emphasis added).

What is your passion? What do you think about most? Which injustice infuriates you? What moves you to tears? That is your calling and your destiny. If you care, God cares even more.

Radical people know they are called, that there is a righteous cause and an upward call that is all encompassing to their life.

> I do not consider brethren, that I have captured and made it my own (yet); but one thing I do – it is my one aspiration: forgetting what lies behind and straining forward to what lies ahead, I press on towards the goal to win the (supreme and heavenly) prize in which God in Christ Jesus is calling us upward.
>
> *Philippians 3:13-14 (AMP)*

> For it is he who delivered us and saved us and <u>called us with a calling</u> in itself holy and leading to holiness; He did it not because of anything of merit that we have done but because of and to further His own purpose...
>
> *2 Timothy 1:9 (AMP, emphasis added)*

> I therefore, the prisoner for the Lord, appeal to and beg you to walk (lead a life) worthy of the divine calling to which you have been called, with behaviour which is a credit to the summons to God's service.
>
> *Ephesians 4:1 (AMP)*

When we find our call we love it! We step into destiny and it satisfies a deep longing and desire within us. It gives us a sense of purpose in our life and an identity. We know *who* we are (which gives us identity) and *whose* we are (which gives us authority). We become a dangerous weapon in the hand of God. We are *"hidden with Christ,"* which is our *"real life"* (Colossians 3:3-4, AMP).

Usually there is one gifting that is outstanding where you succeed most and that others recognize in you. Our gift will always make room for us as we stay surrendered to the will of God in obedience.

How Are We Called?

Most people who are aware of a calling or destiny in God (that is a bit more than attending a nice church, having a nice family, owning a nice house and a nice car etc.) have usually felt a sort of "differentness" about themselves. This causes them to feel that they don't quite fit or belong. This relates particularly to those with a prophetic call. Often there have been unusual amounts of fear or sickness or attempts to simply cause a die-off in the soul, in those who simply know that there is more in God than the present status quo.

Dr. Bill Hamon in his book "Prophets, Apostles and the Coming Moves of God" says:

> "A person receives a divine call from God usually by revelation, knowledge, a vision, a dream, a deep conviction or personal prophecy or prophetic presbytery."

In my own experience, I had always been a small, dreamy child with few friends, a highly developed imagination and a penchant for solitude, fairies and graveyards. For most of my childhood I lived in a large country town in Australia, where I spent large amounts of time either in the library reading, at home writing and drawing, or tearing around the countryside unsupervised with whichever bunch of kids would allow me in.

Brought up in an atheistic family, I was forbidden to go anywhere near a church, so I had little opportunity to access anything of God. My father died suddenly when I was sixteen, and I went on a diligent search for God, attending church services in every single church in town, including the Christadelphians. They locked the door as their service began, which did nothing for my fears. I did not find Him anywhere.

It was to be another ten years (full of everything the world could offer me, including a disastrous marriage to a violent alcoholic in my teens, followed by a divorce leaving me as a single mother with a toddler) before God's intense and pursuing, relentless love arrested me in a moment of His incredible grace and my enormous need. Nothing has ever been the same. During the next ten to twenty years I discovered the beauty of Jesus and the adoration of the Father. I also discovered I had been given a fairly steady gift of prophecy, a passion for Jesus, and a strong desire to see people healed of emotional wounding of all kinds. In my naiveté, I assumed everyone was the same as me. Wrong!

It was not until the 90s that I attended a wonderful prophetic school; still seen, back then, as quite a radical departure from normal Christianity. On the first day, the director of the school prophesied my calling as a prophet and "set me apart" by prayer and impartation. I had an open vision on that day as well, of being taken by the hand by Jesus away from a social gathering, having a pleasant picnic on a river bank in the summer sunshine, and sent to school. It has certainly been an education thus far and I am continually learning. There have been other confirmations by other prophets over the years, but I, like many others, often chose to hide my gifting and calling, probably through lack of confidence and fear of rejection, instead of embracing a gifting which carries responsibility and much obedience. Many waters under many bridges in many countries bring me now to this day.

> Those whom He foreordained He also called; and those whom He called He also justified.
>
> *Romans 8:30 (AMP)*

There are as many ways to be "called of God" as there are various types of "calls". God is the selector, and although He has no favourites, we all have a part to play in the great unfolding of it all. I believe that *"many are called and few are chosen"* (Matthew 20:16, 22:14) means not everyone allows God to apprehend them for the high call. In both these scriptures Jesus alludes to attitude and preparation. We need both for God to commission and send us. We must stay faithful to the end in our calling and our commissioning.

> ...these with Him and on His side are chosen and called, loyal and faithful followers.
>
> *Revelation 17:14 (AMP)*

Ways and Types of Callings

1. Jeremiah was called before birth by God (Jeremiah 1:5).
2. John the Baptist was called before birth by an angel of God (Luke 1:15).
3. David was called by Prophet Samuel (1 Samuel 16:13).
4. Gideon was called by the angel of the Lord (Judges 6:12).
5. Samson was called before birth by an angel (Judges 13:5).
6. Moses was called by the audible voice of God (Exodus 3:4).
7. Joseph was called in a dream (Genesis 37:5).
8. Samuel was called by the audible voice of God (1 Samuel 3:10).

Prophets: The Servants of God

> Surely the Lord will do nothing without revealing His secret to His servants the prophets.
>
> *Amos 3:7 (ESV)*

Prophets are most importantly the servants of God. It is not enough to have a great anointing operating without the character of God. It is more than enough to be anointed and have the character and attitudes of God being worked, or should I say *ground*, in.

> Whatever may be your task, work at it heartily (from the soul), as [something done] for the Lord and not for men.
>
> *Colossians 3:23 (AMP)*

Prophets, in particular, seem to have to deal severely with their own character. I believe part of the reason for this is that Jesus wants to be portrayed in as much truth and purity as we demonstrate in our lives.

> The substance of the truth revealed by Jesus is the spirit of all prophecy.
>
> *Revelation 19:10b (AMP)*

It is vital that we point to Him and not to ourselves. True service lies in being content with obscurity. When life crashes off its axis and all we were once known for in "our" prophetic ministry crashes for whatever reason, it is then that we will meet our fear of obscurity (i.e. will anyone remember me when all this is over?) There are many trips to the Cross, where life and death exist together. Our death – His life.

Jesus redefined greatness with a basin and a towel (John 13:1-17).

> Let this same attitude and purpose and [humble] mind be in you which was in Christ Jesus: [Let Him be your example in humility...]
>
> *Philippians 2:5 (AMP)*

Extrovert prophets will need to deal with their need to be noticed, acknowledged and seen. Introverted prophets will need to deal with intimidation and rejection.

Jesus sought the will and pleasure of His Father and understood completely that He was able to do nothing of Himself independently (John 5:30). We need to do the same. In John 5:30 Jesus depicted servanthood in saying, *"I am able to do nothing from Myself [independently, of my own accord – but only as I am taught by God and as I get His orders] ... I do not seek ... my own will [I have no desire to do what is pleasing to Myself, My own aim, My own purpose] but only the will and pleasure of the Father Who sent Me."* (AMP)

> He who speaks on his own authority seeks to win honor for himself. [He whose teaching originates with himself seeks his own glory.] But He Who seeks the glory and is eager for the honor of Him Who sent Him...
>
> *John 7:18 (AMP)*

> Jesus said to them, My food (nourishment) is to do the will (pleasure) of Him Who sent Me and to accomplish and completely finish His work.
>
> *John 4:34 (AMP)*

To walk as a prophet or prophetic minister in God is to understand the servant heart of Jesus the Prophet. We must release our need to control, our craving to have status, and our need to be right. We must learn how to live in a degree of self-denial where we are not compelled to have our own way all the time.

What if I Refuse my Call?

> For God's gifts and His call are irrevocable. [He never withdraws them once they are given and He does not change His mind about those to whom He gives His grace or to whom He sends His call].
>
> *Romans 11:29 (AMP)*

Even those who have operated mightily in a particular anointing but, through a thousand different circumstances, have plunged into areas that have led them off the main path are able, after repentance and restoration, to pick up the call of God again and go on.

This makes us wiser and stronger and with a deeper understanding of our own frailties and the depth of grace and undeserved favour of God. All this can happen and does, often to the irritation of some of the religious, who can sometimes deeply resent the comeback and restoration. God's grace is incredible and wins me over – always. Fortunately *"mercy triumphs over judgement"* (James 2:13, NIV). If men and women who have fallen into a hole for a season, often publicly and with great repercussions in both families and churches, are willing to address these weaknesses in themselves, all things are again possible in God.

Satan only has access to what we hide in the dark and, like the old-fashioned photo processing, it is in the dark that our negatives are developed. If there are hooks for him to hook to, whether in generational iniquities or weaknesses of our own flesh, he seems to wait for the right moment to enter the doors that have never been shut. Satan is a legalist, an "evil genius", and if there is a legal right to occupy an area he will. It also seems that he will store up an assignment or accusation from the past to wait for an opportune time to attack when it will do the most amount of damage to our ministry. I am pretty sure God gives us many warnings – and a long leash.

We would probably not pick ourselves but, amazingly, God does. If your life has been about disqualification, falling, failing and generally stuffing up, you will be an ideal candidate for God to show His glory in. God will always see to it that what we have been called to do is way beyond our natural capabilities, as He puts out our natural lights so His supernatural light can be seen. We will never be good enough, wise enough, rich enough, tough enough, influential enough or anything enough – but as we decrease, He will increase.

Nothing shall be impossible for God to do through us as we surrender our fears, our inhibitions, our weaknesses and frailties, and let Him out of the box – for us to speak, to decree, to declare, to love, to heal, to sing, to laugh and embrace the world in a holy hug.

God is the ultimate dream-catcher. If you throw your call, your ministry, your dream, God catches it and stores it up for you – for later when the time is right.

Jonah was the classic example of the prophet running from his call, and we will find there are many "whale-belly" experiences for us as holes to fall in on the way. Like Elijah, Jonah despaired and wanted to die when things went in a different way from the plan.

Even though Jonah was furious that God spared the City of Nineveh, God was gracious and merciful to him, asking him in Jonah 4:4, *"Do you do well to be angry?"* (AMP) Jonah went off to sulk and even then God was loving and kind, giving him a shady vine while he stayed in his angry mood. God knows exactly where we are at any time whether it is in a pit or on a mountaintop. He never turns His face away, but it is always easier in the long run to simply say, "Yes Lord! I hear the call, I accept the call, I embrace my call. Whatever is required of me I will do." In that moment of sincere surrender God takes us at our word. Then the tests begin.

We need to *"...note and appreciate the gracious kindness and the severity of God"* (Romans 11:22, AMP). The goodness is shown in the release of His gifts, and the severity is displayed in the process of severe training to prepare us for the commissioning to our calling. The higher the call, the deeper the foundations need to be. Get ready to disappear from the public eye if this is you.

...we must share His suffering if we are to share His glory.

Romans 8:17 (AMP)

A man's gift makes room for him, and brings him before great men.

Proverbs 18:18 (NIV)

Ask yourself: "What is my passion? Where am I most fruitful? What is most prominent in my prophetic words? What gives me most joy? Which injustice provokes me to action?" The answers to these questions point to where your calling lies. And you will love it. This is destiny. This is God!

CHAPTER THREE

The Anointing, Function and Personality of the Prophet

Are You an Emerging Prophet?

The church, in general, is changing gears, and in some instances the entire vehicle is being scrapped for the new model. There is much transition happening everywhere and the leaving of the old traditions of man for the new, fresh-as-manna ways of God. I believe there is an alignment coming to the body of Christ, and the Holy Spirit is the chiropractor so we will not be disjointed, let alone dismembered.

However, God has always had a passion to raise up leaders who walk with a limp from a God-encounter that has brought their strengths and weaknesses to the cross. Our strengths can be as big an impediment to us as our weaknesses. Anything of worth in God will have a cost, and usually the currency is our life.

Probably one of the biggest problems in ministries today is that of stewardship versus ownership. Our ministry (which is actually not, in effect, ours) is simply that of Christ flowing out of us to others. Don't be overawed by the big golden "M" – and I am not talking about fast food.

All may prophesy but not all are prophets. There is a difference between a prophet called "to the office of" and a person with a strong prophetic gifting.

Probably the main qualifications for any emerging minister of any kind are servanthood and humility.

Read the Signs

I believe that there are certain signs that indicate the emergence of a young (not necessarily of age) prophet. The first indicator is a burning passion for God no matter what and relentless pursuit of intimacy.

An emerging prophet will totally surrender to God in humility. He or she allows God to purge, correct, discipline, readjust and kill off whatever character flaws He sees, to develop the heart of the true prophet, the servant of God (Amos 3:7) and all that entails. The formation of the character of God will always be more vital than the gifting itself!

An emerging prophet should have a demonstrated love for the church, the body of Jesus. If a person is truly called into prophetic office I believe he/she must demonstrate an ability to relate and communicate within the church, as well as those outside in the market place, as Jesus did. It is an imbalance to love the Head without loving the body. Jesus does not dismember Himself. This is a vertical and horizontal relationship.

Many churches reject the prophetic, mainly because for a long time it has appeared to be fraught with danger, and lacked integrity. Many prophets have rejected the church too, because of lack of understanding and rejection and abuse. Much healing is needed across many people groups.

If we are genuinely called by God to a people group, particularly a marginalized one, the favour of God will rest more heavily on us as we accept and love those we are amongst in the same way He does. We need to be relatable to whatever culture we find ourselves in. We need a desire and a moving towards being healed from old wounds. It is essential that an emerging prophet pursues his/her journey of healing, or the gifting will not portray Jesus correctly as He is.

Unhealed prophets can tend to be angry, judgmental and critical of the church, leadership and authority. We all need to learn how to walk through rejection with a clean heart.

There should be a constant developing of the gift of prophecy that brings revelation, exhortation and a release in the spirit beyond the average Sunday morning encouragement word to the congregation.

There will be fruit in evidence from the words prophesied. Emerging prophets need to remember that the *"spirits of the prophets are under the speaker's control and subject to being silenced as may be necessary"* (1 Corinthians 14:32-33, AMP). You can contain a prophetic word for as long as it is necessary. If you do not get to release the Word, then you can trust God that it was either wrong timing or that someone else will bring it.

There will be a sense of hope, faith and a charge of life released when a prophet prophesies. People will "know" that "God is in the house".

A prophet is always able to release the gifting, and people should always feel encouraged and loved when a prophet prophesies.

There will constantly be a demonstration of revelation in truth, in the Word of God, in circumstances, in the exposure of hidden truth.

There will be a passion and fervency for truth and justice to prevail. This is the heart of God. Prophets are called to demonstrate the heart of God in every area of righteousness. Some of the questions that need to be asked are: Is it accurate? Does it inspire? Is it coming through a clean heart?

There will be a gradual pervading persuasion from God that the prophetic call is intensifying and encompassing this emerging prophet, as well as a confirmation from others.

Prophets tend to be black and white, no frills, no grey, and there may not be much room for the humanness of people, because there can be very high expectations of people and specifically when it comes to repentance. Prophets can be intolerant of sin – theirs and everyone else's – and can often be quite judgmental. They love the absoluteness of truth and cannot understand why others are so apathetic about God and His Word. They need mentoring into grace, love and relatability as they learn to love the church as Jesus does.

The emerging prophet can be very hard on him/herself, often in condemnation over seeming failures that anybody else would simply shrug off. They need to be mentored towards seeing the heart of the person who "missed the mark" and not concentrate on what was done, but why it was done.

Often prophets are very bold in the anointing but quite insecure in their other areas. They can hear for everyone else but can miss it by a country mile in their own life. We usually have to live what we proclaim. It is the boldness that comes from brokenness that the Lord is after. Prophets are frequently either idolized or rejected or both, in that order.

Our performance orientation needs to die quietly. Unconditional love and acceptance will always win over judgement and law. As parents, when our children lose money, crash a car, or generally mess up their lives we still have a relationship and, hopefully, maintain our love for them. God always loves without conditions, and is always happy and at peace. One of the greatest breakthroughs I have ever learned, that personally assisted my own soul healing, was the knowledge that God was *not* angry with me and even on my worst stuff-up day He remained full of grace and love towards me. Phew!

An emerging prophet needs good mentoring and to be encouraged not to "go to the cave" like a hibernating bear, or at least not stay there for longer than necessary.

Finding good mentoring is about finding someone who is either a prophet or who actually understands you and your prophetic call and who is at least a few metres ahead of you in the race. This is not always easy to find but worth the search, even if it is by email or phone. I have had some excellent mentoring myself and have now mentored quite a few emerging prophets. I offer them all my mistakes and recognition of the holes I fell into, for them to learn from. Perhaps that is one of the reasons God allowed it in the first place.

Good mentoring, I believe, is about ongoing relationship, encouragement and moving people further down the track than you have gone. I prefer to use the word "mentoring" or "friendship" rather than "accountability", as I feel "accountability" denotes a sort of "reporting in" type of behaviour reminiscent of the headmaster's office.

Prophets and prophetic people are often exhausted by the press of people and need to be alone with God often on the mountaintop. There has been a piranha "feeding frenzy" over the years to hear the prophetic word when the prophet is in town. But be assured only God is to have the glory. People who are desperate for a prophetic word often need a healing of their intimacy with God. Every battle we face will be about the battle for intimacy. When we spend enough time simply in the Lord's presence, we will hear Him.

Prophets are called to speak from God to the people, so must spend quality time seeking His face. They need the balance of relatability in the form of fellowship with less intense Christians, and even those with completely different gifts and callings. This, I believe, is vital for balance.

A good teaching prophet will teach the people how to access God and hear for themselves.

Characteristics of Prophets

1. Have you ever watched the "sniffer dogs" at the airport sniffing at people's baggage looking for fruit? They are focused on the job at hand and are not looking for pats on the head or conversation with random customers. They are like prophets at work. Prophets are <u>here to announce, point, discern, and "sniff out"</u> Jezebel, manipulation, fear, control and religion – which are all enemies of the prophet.

2. <u>Always wants to adjust and bring justice.</u> Repentance is a top priority.

3. <u>Ceaselessly toiling, microscopic, and sensitive.</u> They like to go alone on the mountain because they need to get alone with God. The prophet does the job, goes home, and tends to become "peopled out" fast.

4. <u>Loves to prophesy,</u> loves to change things in the spirit realm.

5. <u>Seems to "peel off covers" and expose situations and areas,</u> and then cuts away until everything is laid bare (e.g. Nathan the Prophet to King David).

6. <u>Often has a tangible anointing.</u>

7. <u>A growing awareness that the heart of the prophet is the heart of God,</u> and that God's prophets down through the centuries are very dear to His heart

Surely the Lord God will do nothing without revealing His secret to His servants the prophets.

Amos 3:7 (AMP)

...do my prophets no harm.

1 Chronicles 16:22 (NIV)

8. Prophets are <u>not interested in religious superficial rituals,</u> only reality, truth and moving things in the spirit realm so that people will see the face of God. Mature, healed prophets always want God to have all the glory, never themselves.

9. <u>They tend to be in or out, on or off.</u> Their yes is yes and their no is no. There are not many "grey areas", in fact not enough. I believe, as I go on, that God seems to be greyer than black and white – with many edges blurred. It's me that can be inflexible. The pastoral anointing has lots of leash, lots of grey, lots of mercy, and is probably more like the Father really. The prophet often exposes unsanctified mercy, which is where mercy is extended when in fact God wants to discipline and mature a person (or even kill something in a life that we want to keep giving life to).

10. Prophets <u>can be ruthless with sin,</u> their own and everyone else's. They can despise weakness but not the weak. In

counselling they give direct truth, and major in deliverance. They will not abide evil in any form. It must go.

11. Prophets are <u>utterly non-compromising, constantly self-evaluating</u>, and can set the bar almost too high until they learn to relax and chill out a whole lot more. Being with an emerging prophet can be very intense and exhausting. There often seems to be no "off" switch.

12. They have <u>the heart of an encourager</u> to release and impart always. People should always feel God's love and encouragement when a prophet ministers, and never threatened or afraid. Fear or feeling threatened is not the heart of Jesus.

13. They are <u>the five senses</u> – smell, touch, hearing, taste and sight – of the Body of Christ. A church trying to push forward without prophetic input will travel very slowly, with short sight.

14. Prophets often <u>have had major assignments from the devil</u>, from birth, and sometimes before birth, to prevent them moving into their calling. There are often years spent in barren wilderness places, as well as episodes of assault with fear and control. It is not unusual to have had a history of abuse and violence to break their will to live.

15. Satan fears prophetic anointing, as it ultimately <u>announces the return of Jesus, exposes strategies, and will not compromise truth</u>. He fears the authority and humility of Jesus. True prophets cannot be bought or sold.

16. Then there is the <u>"Jeremiah" anointing</u> (Jeremiah 1:10) that roots out, pulls down, destroys, overthrows, then builds and plants. This is an essential anointing and belongs to an apostolic prophet, called to overthrow the existing status quo in the spiritual realm and establish God's Kingdom in a place. Sometimes this anointing can be misconstrued as anger or unhealed wounds, and as possible as this may be, it

is more often than not a focused intensity as the prophet listens to God and does His bidding.

There is intentionality with the prophet that is the heart of God to probe, expose and destroy, often with surgical precision. This anointing of God pulls down walls, hindrances, and kicks down doors. The Jeremiah-type prophet uproots religiosity and exposes false doctrine, logic, error and humanistic philosophy. They overthrow existing evil in a place, and brings light into shadowy places. These prophets build people not ministries. They are Kingdom-minded not ministry-minded. They plant people and churches.

The Jeremiah 1:10 anointing is about apostolic prophets, those called to build and equip in many regions, churches and nations. They *"correctly [handle] the word of truth"* (2 Timothy 2:15, NIV). In fact, the Word of God is very dear to the heart of the prophet.

Jeremiah had to first allow God to deal with his self-perception, his youthfulness, and his fear. In the same way Elijah had to deal with his depression and fear, as did Gideon. Jonah was shown his anger and rebellion. This was so that God could use them even more effectively. We all have our issues but God always sees and speaks potential, seeing the gold in the dirt. We need to do the same, with ourselves and each other and any that God sends us to.

17. A developing prophet often <u>questions every part of the spoken Word,</u> and often speaks to the preacher after the meeting to understand exactly what was meant.

18. A prophet <u>may perceive the negatives in character, motives and heart of a person,</u> but be restrained by God from doing anything about it except pray. Like everyone else, prophets must continually put on love. They certainly can't see everything in a person, only what God shows. The more discretion you show in keeping confidences the more God

will trust you with. Many people avoid spending time with prophets because they fear their whole lives are laid open to view. Prophets need to spend time with people with opposite anointings and learn to chill out and have some fun, or they become too intense.

19. There will be an <u>urgent desire to see</u> the same <u>brokenness</u> in people that has been wrought by God in them. They are often ruthless with sin, their own and everyone else's, and love to see an outward manifestation of inward conviction.

20. <u>Rejection and fear are two of the biggest enemies</u> of prophets and prophetic people. They are very sensitive to slightest rejection, thoughts, attitudes, very tuned in to the moods and attitudes of others, having emotional radars a mile long.

21. Prophets with a calling to other people groups, other nations, are often <u>more interested in establishing Kingdom principles</u> in a place, town or nation <u>than in the individual problems and plans of people</u>. These are the apostolic prophets who are far-sighted, already seeing into next year. They live in the present, looking at the future, and rarely in the past. They are planning and strategizing continually. They are "Kingdom-minded", not so much interested in the individual or the details involved in getting there.

Prophets never really take enough breaks, often feeling it is unnecessary. So they'll work until midnight and start again at dawn, driven with an urgent awareness of times and seasons. It is like fiery embers smouldering on the inside, always ready, always alert, hearing the voice of God constantly and never quite switching off.

Most prophets who are mature and desire to walk in humility are not interested in everyone *knowing* they are a prophet but simply want Jesus to be seen. It is desirable, though, that a prophet is acknowledged as such by other ministers, and the calling is endorsed, so that there is no constraint in the prophet functioning freely in the house of God, or wherever they are called to go.

The call finds us and chooses us. Many are called but not all pick it up. Once we accept the prophetic call from God and embrace it, it is like a coat that is too big for us initially but we learn to grow into it and love to wear it. Ephesians 4:11-13 is the "some but not all" scripture. This talks about the five-fold gifting from God of apostles, prophets, evangelists, pastors and teachers. These men and women are the "body builders" of the church, the consultants, the trainers who are in the church to focus on preparing God's people *"for works of service, so that the body of Christ may be built up..."* (verse 12, NIV) The work is often slow and impeded, unacknowledged and replaced by programmes, meetings and more meetings.

The prophetic ministry is designed to work alongside (not beneath or above) the other five-fold ministers *"until we all reach unity in the faith"* (NIV).

In God's order, the prophetic gift works not in opposition to but alongside others, to compliment them, not thinking more highly of itself than of others. It is often resisted by those who, to quote Bob Dylan, "criticize what we don't understand".

Prophetic ministry exposes idolatry in church. Whatever you think about most is your god. Your ministry (which is actually God's not yours) and your gifting can become an idol. There can be an urgent and ungodly desire for a ministry rooted in the need for recognition. We don't have to worry, though, as God has perfect ways to bring it toppling down, along with our dear selves, from our pedestal of adulation that we have allowed people to put us upon.

We could probably all say we are tired of abuse and wary of it. Many of God's prophets and prophetic ministers and musicians have been in wilderness areas for years. Today's prophetic musicians and worshippers have not come from palaces and places of grandeur but their long preparation time has been in the cave of Adullum with their King. They have been in the desert, the wilderness, invisible, forgotten seemingly by man, hidden away under God's shadow, being prepared for such a time as this. They have learnt to be hand-fed by the ravens and nurtured on little. The Adullum dwellers are coming out – albeit dishevelled and with a limp – but they are coming from the back blocks to the front.

Prophetic musicians and worshippers simply want to worship at His feet, want no claim, no fame, no name so that God gets all the glory.

They have allowed Him to burn His seal into their spirit and to ravish their hearts. They have allowed Him to mould them on the potter's wheel, sometimes screaming to be allowed to get off. They know rejection. In fact sometimes their behaviour has been labelled rebellion as they resist control and conditioning for it destroys their anointing. They have become vagabonds in the spirit, following the King to the ends of the earth on a quest for freedom in worship.

They have often suffered abuse of every form, misunderstanding, slander and gossip and accusation, but keep coming back to the King's embrace of love and restoration.

The Importance of Character in Prophetic Ministry

For too long the church has confused anointing with character.

We need to look for fruit and not become impressed only with gifting. When we see the gift, the gift itself is not necessarily an indication of character alone. Everyone can look attractive under the anointing of God because of His beauty, not necessarily ours. People always need to meet Jesus in us. We may be the only demonstration of Him they may ever meet so it is important to represent Him and His character in a true way.

The Word of God talks of *"sin's deceitfulness"* (Hebrews 3:13, NIV). The deceit is that we think God overlooks it. He doesn't, we just have a long leash, but when we repent it is covered.

We are instructed in Romans 12:6, *"...if your gift is prophesying, then prophesy in accordance with your faith..."* (NIV) Don't go beyond what the Lord is saying. His words must be in our mouth, not our words in our mouth. Prophets know that their mouth is the Lord's.

We do not convert people to our church, our movement or ourselves but to Jesus, or we are being false in our intentions before God. Jesus is not a good idea but the only way. It is not so much that He is in control, but rather that He reigns with His character and majesty. We need to build into people not organizations; it's not how much you are doing, but how much of Jesus can be seen in you. Remember that many have been wounded by unhealed prophets, but just as many by unhealed pastors, teachers, evangelists and leaders of all sorts. We are still making a lot of relational mistakes. Our hope has to be in God rather than people. He will never disappoint.

If we lose our "first love" we have lost everything for He *is* love. As I build upon my first love, my love for Him increases, because I know Him more now.

Jesus *is* the purpose. He doesn't lead to it, He *is* it.

Finding Rest

> My people have become lost sheep, their shepherds have led them astray ... they have gone from mountain to hill and have forgotten their resting place.
>
> *Jeremiah 60:6 (NIV)*

If you keep people excited and moving from one project to another you deprive them of rest and development of intimacy. This all becomes hype rather than true zeal for God. Hype is artificial stimulation. The church is worn out from over-programming. If you're a leader, the best thing you can do for your people is stay under the shadow of the Almighty. The shadow *is* the overshadowing of Christ. It is His overshadowing wing that heals, speaks, restores. He'll do the rest.

Jesus tells us to, *"...take My yoke upon you ... you will find rest ... for your souls."* (Matthew 11:29, AMP)

Prophetic Personality

Where you find prophets you find hunger. You also usually find rejection and insecurity. Learn to live with your prophetic anointing and its intensity, but learn to switch it off and let your soul live.

The pastoral, evangelistic and teaching giftings are people-gifts, and include plenty of cups of tea, lots of chats, lots of mercy counselling sessions. We all need each other's giftings from time to time.

Be mentored in your gifting and your life. Hang with people who are further ahead and know more. Don't run with loopy, flaky, weak fools. You will tend towards the weaknesses and the strengths of whomever leads and mentors you.

Most prophets hate rules and religion, committees and meetings for the sake of meetings, and are often seen as rebellious, but they have a desire for reality and truth. They are "no frills" people. Prophets, like everyone else though, need to learn to submit to godly authority and simply be part of a local church.

Prophets are microscopic, have antennae fifty metres long, and detect changes in atmospheres, so they can then change it by their own anointing. They generally only have a few trusted friends, who actually understand them and love them.

Prophets have different equipment to work with than the other five-fold ministers. Accuracy will always make people afraid. God judges the prophetic office quickly.

They are often quiet, sensitive people who respond to how God is feeling. Minor things to non-prophetic people can be major to a prophet.

Walking through Rejection

...if I were still seeking the popularity of men I would not be the bondservant of Christ.

Galatians 1:10 (AMP)

...God is not impressed with the positions that men hold...

Galatians 2:6 (AMP)

> ...for men to seek glory, their glory, causes suffering.
>
> *Proverbs 25:27 (AMP)*

Rejection always accompanies true ministry. To handle rejection without being offended is a mark of maturity, which is Christ-likeness. Few things test our patterning after Him like rejection. Broken vessels understand grace. God wants us to find the place where we surrender our reaction, surrender what has happened, so we can never blame people or circumstances. Ultimately forgiveness is being able to no longer blame anybody, including God, and being able to say, "Nobody owes me anything." Give God the "Rod of Judgement".

I believe God would have us pursue reconciliation where there has been a break in relationship wherever it is possible. However if we pursue those who simply won't forgive, we can end up in the same black, imprisoning hole that they are in. In this case we simply move on, using the situation as fertilizer for the next growth.

Character Sketches

Old Testament prophets are often seen as an extreme. New Testament prophets need to be totally real, totally loving of people, without judgement, totally approachable, fun to be with, lovers of God. In fact, they are to be like who Jesus really is.

Prophets are called to comfort the afflicted and afflict the comfortable.

Prophesying is not a license to beat people with judgement and condemnation. Teaching is not a license to show people how right you are and how much you know. Counselling is not a license to fill your need to be needed.

We need a soft, tender heart to speak *His* words. We should not find it easy to give harsh words or we are coming from a wrong spirit indicative of unattended wounds.

Examples of Different Anointing and Character of Old Testament Prophets

SAMSON:

He had a residual weakness for the wrong women but a huge, crushing, violent anointing. He had a faulty character, and lost his eyes (vision) and worked for another man's vision, leading to slavery and captivity. Un-wholeness often attracts to itself, and we can be drawn to the same level of dysfunction as ourselves. When we are young, we can find that too many hormones and too much time is a bad combination. You can end up with the wrong partner through loneliness rather than the will of God and waiting for "the right one".

GIDEON:

He was soft, gentle, timid and a melancholy personality, representative of the anointing of the 70s known as the charismatic renewal. He described himself as "least of least" (indicating he had an inferiority complex) but God prophesied his potential. His courage built up as prophetic anointing came.

> ...the spirit of the Lord clothed Gideon with Himself and took possession of him, and he blew a trumpet...
>
> *Judges 6:34 (AMP)*

JONAH:

He was constantly running from his call, and gave into self-pity when God saved people and did not destroy them. He had a melancholy personality and was weak in character.

SAMUEL:

He was called and separated early, and sacrificed to God by a godly mother.

Raised under Priest Eli, Samuel is representative of the prophetic movement whereas Eli represents the negative qualities of the old pastoral movement, which was deaf to the voice of the Lord, blind to the new move of God, fat from greed and prosperity, refusing to discipline the immorality of the staff, leading to a total fall of a whole family (three generations lost in one day).

Samuel constantly pointed to a higher person. He fell into the trap of looking to the outer person, though, when selecting the king who would succeed Saul (1 Samuel 16:6).

In 1 Samuel 3:19 it says that *"the Lord was with him and let none of his words fall to the ground"* (AMP). Samuel set up prophetic schools as God released His prophets at that time to be His voice to the nation.

Elijah:

This is the prophet of fire, who began his ministry and was then hidden away by God in the wilderness, where he learned the fullness of God's amazing provision, fed by the ravens at the brook Cherith. He had an amazing encounter with Jezebel and the prophets of Baal, whom he slew in a display of the majesty of God. He also trained schools of prophets and left a legacy behind him. When the news came to him that Jezebel was after him to kill him, he fell into depression and fear – and who could blame him? – and God had to come and bail him out from his place of self-defence and isolation. He was taken into heaven by a whirlwind and accompanied by angels of fire and chariots of fire (2 Kings 2:11).

Elisha:

Elisha was trained under Elijah and followed him right up to his amazing removal from earth in a whirlwind. He followed him closely and asked for a double portion of Elijah's fire anointing, which he received.

His first prophetic mantle came on him as he was going about his daily duties in the field and God asked him if he was prepared to burn his plough. Sometimes we will be asked to give up what our usual career/income is to serve God and trust Him for His provision. He always pays for what He orders.

Elisha's acts of God were greater in number with many signs following, but it is Elijah – and the Elijah anointing on God's end-time prophetic company – that God speaks of through the prophet Malachi.

> Behold, I will send you Elijah the prophet before the coming of the great and dreadful day of the LORD: And he shall turn the heart of the fathers to the children, and the heart of the children to their fathers...
>
> *Malachi 4:5-6a (KJV)*

MOSES:

Moses was rescued from a holocaust type of ethnic cleansing, then was educated and instructed in palatial surroundings in the ways of the Egyptians, but chose to obey the call of God and be identified with the affliction of his own people.

As great as all these Old Testament prophets were, in James 5:17 it says that *"Elijah was a human being with a nature such as we have [with feelings, affection and a constitution like ours]..."* (AMP) God gifts whomever He likes and we find Jesus in some unusual places (like in ourselves, for example).

We may suffer abuse of every form, misunderstanding, slander and gossip and accusation, and even betrayal, but as long as we keep coming back to the King's embrace of love and restoration, our journey continues.

CHAPTER FOUR

Prophets in Training (P.I.T.s)

The time between the calling and the release is the preparation time. This is where God deals with the motives of our heart. When we think we are ready, we are usually not, I have discovered along the way.

Biblical Examples of Training of Prophets

- Moses, rescued from holocaust type "ethnic cleansing", was educated and instructed in the ways of the Egyptians, but chose to obey the call of God and to be identified with the affliction of his own people.

- Samuel, the child birthed through the prayer of his mother, given to God under the training of Eli, whose own family were undisciplined and disobedient... Samuel set up Prophetic Schools as God released His prophets at that time to be His voice to the nation.

- Elijah began his ministry and then was hidden away by God, fed by ravens at the brook Cherith, came up against Jezebel and slew eight hundred and fifty of her false prophets, and had an amazing public prophetic ministry. He fell into deep depression when he heard that Jezebel was after him, and God had to draw him from his cave and send him on to his next mission. This included finding and setting apart Elisha, his next apprenticed prophet. Elijah also trained schools of prophets.

- <u>Elisha</u>, trained under Elijah, pressed in closely and received his mantle as Elijah was taken up to heaven.

The Main Areas of Attack

OUR PERSONAL LIFE:

I am speaking of the quiet, hidden places and those that may be hidden in the dark. God has a way of probing them open into light so that they may be healed.

OUR FAMILY:

It appears that if the devil can't quite get through to us he will attack our children or those closest to our heart.

OUR FRIENDS:

Missed communication is often rife between those we call our friends and us. Division is a speciality of the devil. He hates unity and all things that promote loving relationship.

OUR FINANCES:

This can be incredibly distracting but also a challenge to trust God as our ultimate provider and not ourselves

OUR MINISTRY:

Of course our ministry is not ours to be concerned about as it is actually a stewardship of the particular garden God has given us to tend. "Ministry" is simply whatever of Jesus flows out of us at any particular time. The idolatry of this particular "golden M" needs to fall into a hole and die quickly, and God has the perfect way for this to happen. Prophets, particularly, are called to exhibit humility and repentance and to ensure that Jesus is seen and heard in every circumstance. All the glory is His alone. We are simply the vessel He dares to use.

Remember, when you recognize that you are under some form of attack, God says the exact opposite of the lie you may believe from the devil. God is totally enamoured of us. The devil will always exaggerate the need for performance, but we need to fully understand that we are always *"accepted in the beloved"* (Ephesians 1:6, KJV). In Ephesians 2:10 (and this is so lovely), He even calls us His poems (from the Greek word "poema"). Our position is that we are actually seated with Him in heavenly places (Ephesians 2:6). Spiritually we are in heaven. We are a spirit, possessing a soul and clothed with a body. Amazing!

Isolation, Wounding and Offence

An isolation spirit is often accompanied by a persecution complex. Ideally we need to be relating in intimate transparent friendship to a couple of trusted friends that we know love us and have our best interests at heart and are wedged into a body of believers. Not an easy find but not impossible either.

Yes, we all have times of being in seclusion, but do not isolate yourself. Jesus took many times out, away from the mob, to spend alone with His Father, to hear and move on.

- *Seclusion* is about privacy and solitude – "to shut off from influence" (Oxford English Dictionary).
- *Isolation* is "to place in a detached situation like an island, to segregate" (Oxford English Dictionary). It has the potential over an extended period to take us into delusion.

Interestingly, we get wounded in relationships but also healed in relationships. Psalm 68:6 says, *"God places the solitary in families..."* (AMP)

Joshua hung around the tent of the glory. We need to do likewise.

We ought to hang with strong, anointed prophetic and apostolic people who know their call and are walking in it and have no desire for worldly pursuits.

I encourage you to read the excellent plethora of great books available, listen to CDs, and worship, worship, worship. Keep being activated. Get with prophetic intercessors; go to conferences, but above all, *spend time with the King.*

We isolate often because of woundedness and misunderstanding. When we are honest, God can heal. We can lose our mind, let alone our ministry, by parking at isolation and feeding our rejections and wounds. Our silent vows of "I will never..." or "I will always..." keeps our wounds open and bleeding. It is a breeding ground for deception and error.

Prophetic people adore Jesus but are tired of abuse and want to be with people who will not wound them further. Simple and basic.

How it Spirals

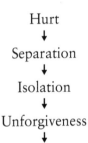

Hurt
↓
Separation
↓
Isolation
↓
Unforgiveness
↓
A root of bitterness is produced,
contaminates the water we swim in
↓
Grief – literally "death comes to the heart"

We can become like our offender through a soul tie of unforgiveness.

Remember, too, that vengeance is only sweet for a season.

The Cure

You may have heard the expression, "We are wounded in community, but we are also healed in community." Listen closely to what God is saying about where to be in community. We desperately need true spiritual communities where we can feel safe enough to tell our story and be accepted with the unconditional love that Jesus has towards us. When we feel safe and loved, our healing will begin. If He accepts us with all our nonsense, who are we not to accept firstly ourselves, then everyone else God sends across our path? The cross is sufficient, even for us. It is a time to look at each other's faces instead of the back of each other's heads!

Finding community is a miracle in itself. It cannot happen without the Holy Spirit and a safe spiritual director who simply is not interested in coercion or control. Building community is slow and painful but worth it all. It is also a rare treasure. Apostolic/ prophetic ministry, particularly if it is itinerant, can be lonely and isolating, and we need to have healthy, normal friendships in community to return home to.

Suspicion creates paranoia and is the opposite of true discernment. Elijah suffered from isolation: "I'm the only one left." If you are called to, "Go ye!" then you can't stay home.

When isolation hits you:

- It puts invisible barriers between you and others through fear of rejection.
- It tells lies and isolates you from friends and family and those you used to trust.
- It creates barrenness, from no intimacy, no duplication.

The Hospital Church, and the Broken Hearted

The word "hospital" originally meant "a hostel for travellers, an institution for the old and infirm or an educational facility for needy children" (Oxford English Dictionary). Of course our word "hospitality" came from the root word. The Knights of St. John, in Malta, built a hospital for pilgrims in Jerusalem during the Crusades of the 11th Century.

I believe the church is many facets in one large global body. One of them needs to be the provision of intensive care for those who are wounded and ill, either physically, emotionally or spiritually. God is currently healing his body, restoring his people, cleansing his bride.

The restoration healing movement started in the 1980s, and the Lord has raised many in this sometimes neglected area. People like John and Paula Sandford who founded Elijah House, Leanne Payne of Pastoral Care Ministries, and Dr. Harold Dewberry, founder of Teen Challenge Australia, are some of my heroes in the faith who have mentored thousands through their books and teaching. The other rail in my own ministry is restoration healing, which I consider essential in the equipping of people everywhere. My utter joy is in teaching schools of restoration healing and seeing God transform broken lives through deep healing and deliverance.

The army of God has sometimes effectively shot itself in the foot while others have shot each other in the back and heart. Wounded soldiers do not go to the frontline. Too often we have shot our own wounded and rendered them even more ineffective. Sometimes we have become cannibalistic and constantly devoured one another.

Many churches are like an army with a hospital corps. I believe it is vital to have as many keys to healing the heart as possible.

Everybody has a story and a right to tell it somewhere safe, to receive the healing and affirmation from the Lord that is their inheritance. A wounded prophet will not portray Jesus adequately in truth.

In a church that is moving in present truth, there may be seasons of being an "Adullum" church, where all the wounded warriors need time to recover. The ideal progression is then to a season as a "Hebron" church, where people are equipped, anointed and strengthened and trained. We can then move into Zion, the city of God. This speaks of governmental ruling in a city and an establishing can come upon the work. It speaks of the apostolic anointing moving on a work, a church, a ministry.

As we take accountability for our own un-wholeness and allow God to heal and restore, we will refuse offence, slander, gossip and accusation of one another so God can raise up his prophetic warriors. We can either bind people with our unforgiveness or loose them with our mercy. If we continue to retain offences, we become like the offender. We are only as sick as our secrets keep us.

> When I kept silence, [before I confessed], my bones wasted away through my groaning ... I acknowledged my sin to you and my iniquity I did not hide. I said I will confess my sin to the Lord [continually unfolding the past until all is told], then you [instantly] forgave me the guilt and iniquity of my sin.
>
> *Psalm 32:3,5 (AMP)*

Open wounds attract flies. When we get rid of garbage the rats leave. We need to know how to handle offence. If we are called to prophetic ministry there will be many opportunities for offence, retaliation, rejection and misunderstanding, and it will be a lifelong challenge to keep a merciful heart and barrel loads of grace.

> I will send you Elijah the prophet before the ... day of the Lord comes.
>
> *Malachi 4:5 (AMP)*

God is raising up a company of prophets in this hour who fear God and terrify the devil through their humility, their surrender to Christ and their accuracy in the word of prophecy.

Handling Offence... or Not

The word "offence" comes from the Greek "scandaliso", where of course the word "scandal" is from. In the Oxford English Dictionary it says, "To shock or offend the moral feelings." Many times Jesus was seen as "scandalous" and an offence to the Pharisees, by the way He acted and spoke. He broke all the rules. He worked on the Sabbath, threw people out, spat on eyes and associated with immoral men and women, the marginalized, the wicked and the sexually depraved. And don't we love Him for all of that?

In Matthew 13 Jesus taught a series of parables that were so loaded with wisdom and insight that everyone was amazed and astounded. He then went to Nazareth and to the synagogue and taught there. Those present were "amazed with bewildered wonder". As you would be! But these people were also offended and wanted to know how on earth someone they had all grown up with, that had had a scandal hanging over his head from before birth, was now expounding wisdom and doing miracles.

Interestingly, they also were *"hindered from acknowledging His authority"* (Matthew 13:57, AMP). Offence will always cause us to distrust those in authority over us. Offence will cause us to see what it is we disapprove of in a person. Jesus says in Luke 7:23, *"Blessed ... is he who takes no offence in Me."* (AMP) It's a good idea not to take on someone else's offence – our own is enough. If you are imprisoned by offence you will not be able to war. A mark of maturity is to realize how long we hold on to offences.

If someone has been offended by us and will not move towards forgiveness and reconciliation, then just let it go and walk on, or you will be drawn down into their black bottomless pit of unforgiveness and bitterness.

> Strive to have a conscience void of offence.
>
> *Acts 24:16 (NIV)*

I think we get the picture.

The Contemplative Life

It is good to develop a contemplative mind which is stayed on Him.

> You will guard him and keep him in perfect and constant peace whose mind [both its inclination and character] is stayed on You, because he commits himself to You, leans on You, and hopes confidently in You.
>
> *Isaiah 26:3 (AMP)*

Contemplation is about realizing that the Lord is in this moment now and it is not an empty moment.

If we don't get this now, we will always be grasping for more and searching for extra, which causes us to be greedy, controlling everybody and manipulating others' lives.

One of my favourite authors is Richard Rohr, a Franciscan priest living amongst the poor in New Mexico. In his book entitled "Everything Belongs" he wrote:

> "True contemplatives are paradoxically risk-takers and reformists, precisely because they have no private agendas, jobs or securities to maintain. Their security and identity is founded in God, not in being right, being paid by a church or looking for promotion in people's eyes ... God is always bigger than the boxes we build for God, so we should not waste too much time protecting the boxes."

Differences between Old Testament Prophets and New Testament Prophets

People should never be afraid of prophets and prophetic ministry. An example of an Old Testament style of prophet is found in 1 Samuel 16:4, where we read, *"...the elders ... trembled at his coming and said, Have you come peaceably?"* (AMP) On the other hand, modern day prophets must be lovers of God, lovers of people, and great encouragers. When a prophet is here, we should feel challenged, encouraged, stretched but *loved*, not berated, beaten up or fearful.

John, the last of the Old Testament prophets, submits his ministry to Jesus, who is the first New Testament prophet, by saying, *"He must increase, but I must decrease"* (John 3:30, AMP).

cannot cut short the preparation time or we will be like a baby born before time and will struggle to survive. The Bible talks of *"the deceitfulness of sin"* (Hebrews 3:13, AMP). The deceit is that we think God overlooks it, but He doesn't; we simply have a long leash.

Why the Wilderness?

Sometimes we go into a wilderness when we are full, and God is well pleased with us, but wants to empty us out for another filling. Most wilderness times feel like a punishment. Other times we might go into a wilderness time because of a stupid mistake, or we have pre-empted God, or been at the brunt of a betrayal. Whatever the reason we need to let God deal and heal and bring us out when He says, not when we think.

Jesus Himself was *"...led (guided) by the [Holy] Spirit into the wilderness (desert) to be tempted (tested and tried) by the devil"* (Matthew 4:1, AMP). Jesus fasted for forty days and was tested and tried, and when He came out, Matthew 4:17 (AMP) says, that *"From that time Jesus began to preach, crying out, Repent (change your mind for the better, heartily amend your ways, with abhorrence of your past sins), for the kingdom of heaven is at hand."*

If we yield to the workings of God in our wilderness time, fasting and seeking God, we will receive revelation and power. It is here that we let everything die, what we thought was "ours": ministry, gifting, opportunities and achievements. This is what gives us an edge to what follows.

Reasons why we go through the wilderness:

- For us to see what is in our hearts when God leans heavily on us in this season of seeming desert. Deuteronomy 8:2 says, *"And you shall ... remember all the way which the Lord your God led you these forty years ... to humble you and to prove you, to know what was in your ... heart, whether you would keep His commandments or not."* (AMP)
- It is during this seemingly dry, barren, non-productive and lonely time that God allows us to hunger and to see that we

are to live *"by every word that proceeds out of the mouth of the Lord"* (Deuteronomy 8:3, AMP).

- To break down our stubbornness and rebellion. When we come out and our captivity is turned and the Promised Land is obtained we must not think that our own righteousness achieved anything. *"Know therefore that the Lord your God does not give you this good land to possess because of your righteousness, for you are a hard and stubborn people."* (Deuteronomy 9:6, AMP).

- To bring us into a place of deep trust, knowing that *"...neither death nor life, neither angels nor demons, neither the present nor the future, nor any powers, neither height nor depth, nor anything else in all creation, will be able to separate us from the love of God that is in Christ Jesus our Lord."* (Romans 8:38-39).

- That we will endure the abandonment by those we thought we could rely on, as Jesus did, but still show grace and forgiveness. *"At my first trial no one acted in my defence, or took my part or even stood with me, but all forsook me. May it not be charged against them!"* (2 Timothy 4:1, AMP).

- That we will know the goodness and severity of the Father heart of God (Romans 11:22).

- So we will simply believe God. *"Therefore beware brethren, take care lest there be in any one of you a wicked, unbelieving heart, refusing to trust in and rely on him – leading you to turn away and stand aloof from the Living God."* (Hebrews 3:12, AMP). It was simply unbelief that shut out the Israelites from the Land (Hebrews 3:19).

- That we will learn to trust that God feeds us in the wilderness. Jesus breaks bread with us "on the way" so that our hunger will be for Him alone. In this moment our eyes are opened.

- That our own agendas are cancelled and we learn to live at rest at the feet of Jesus.

There comes a time when waters are eventually found in the wilderness.

> For waters shall gush forth in the wilderness, and streams in the desert.
>
> *Isaiah 35:6 (NIV)*

> I will make rivers flow on barren heights, and springs within the valleys. I will turn the desert into pools of water, and the parched ground into springs.
>
> *Isaiah 41:18 (NIV)*

When we are in a pit, and if we keep digging in, we will find water. No one but God sees you digging. Like trench warfare, don't put your head up until the command. The well of the Word you have dug in your life is for you to drink from in the dry season. The *"rivers of living water"* (John 7:38, AMP) are for others to drink from, particularly when we minister to people prophetically. If you have not dug a well, you have to drink from someone else's, but your well is with you wherever you go. It needs to be filled and replenished all the time. We often have to remove the debris from our well so there will be no pollution of the water. The river that comes out of your innermost being is for everyone to drink from, swim in.

A drink of sparkling, cold water is an encouragement in a dry place. The devil prowls around like a beast of prey and targets those who are weary, weak or wounded. This is why we need to encourage one another every day. Learn to be a Barnabas (a son of encouragement) and keep the bar open twenty-four hours a day. A cool drink is appreciated by those who are thirsty, not the saturated.

On the other hand, the unrighteous ones are described in 2 Peter 2:17 as *"springs without water and mists driven along before a tempest"* (AMP). We are not to poison another man's well with bitterness, contention, hostility or accusation.

> He turns the wilderness into a pool of water, and dry ground into water springs.
>
> *Psalm 107:35 (AMP)*

> Passing through the Valley of Weeping (Baca), they make it a place of springs; the early rain also fills [the pools] with blessings.
>
> *Psalm 84:6 (AMP)*

We need to dig wells as a heritage for our next generation, as Abraham did for Isaac. As we unstop the wells of the preceding generation we need to "undig" the old generational iniquities so we can pass on a godly heritage to our children and our grandchildren. If we teach our own children the ways of God, our grandchildren will be born with a disposition towards righteousness. If we do not, our grandchildren are born with rebellion in their hearts.

> If your children will keep My covenant and My testimony that I shall teach them, their children also shall sit upon your throne forever.
>
> *Psalm 132:12 (AMP)*

In Exodus 15:23 we read, *"When they came to Marah, they could not drink its waters for they were bitter..."* (AMP) When the waters are bitter we need to place a tree of forgiveness in so the waters will be sweet.

Song of Solomon 4:12 speaks of when we are *"a garden enclosed and barred ... a spring shut up, a fountain sealed"* (AMP). God wants to gush forth from out of our innermost being, and we cannot speak out His words or His songs until our fountain is released, our wounds healed and the fear of man is removed from us and we can cry with our whole heart, *"All my fountains are in You."* (Psalm 87:7, NIV).

How to Wait

> Yes, let none who trust and wait hopefully and look for You be put to shame or be disappointed.
>
> *Psalm 25:3 (AMP)*

> My soul, wait only upon God and silently submit to Him; for my hope and expectation are from Him.
>
> *Psalm 62:5 (AMP)*

The waiting time is the conditioning time.

Prophetic words come from The Word (Bible) and the prophetic Word (the "rhema word" or the "logos word"). We agree with the word about our life, our ministry, our call – and life then appears to go in the opposite direction to the word prophesied. This is the testing time, the waiting time, and the conditioning time. This is where the devil comes as he did to Eve and whispers, "Hath God said? Are you sure it was God?" We are flooded with doubt, fear and unbelief. Our circumstances scream at us. Our marriage, our ministry, our morality, our integrity are stretched and blitzed beyond our comprehension. Our children's lives fall apart and we question everything we ever thought we knew about God, His Word, His character. All that is left is the call on our lives, God, His faithfulness, and His Word.

When we are utterly convinced that no good thing could possibly come out of us and we are a million eons from ready, God says, "Perfect! Ready! Let's go." And you do. If you choose to.

The Waiting Room

Like waiting in the delivery room at the Maternity Hospital, we cannot hurry the natural progression of things. God is never late. He will not come on our time. If we truly trust God with "our times" and can say, *"My times are in [His] hands"* (Psalm 31:15, NIV), His purposes will come to pass as we surrender each moment, obey the last instruction until we get the next one, and trust, trust, trust that we can *"be still and know that [He] is God"* (Psalm 46:10, NIV) and is working *all things* together for good for those who love Him (Romans 8:28). We cannot orchestrate the fulfilment of prophecy by any means other than waiting on God and trusting in Him to *"[watch] over [His] word to perform it"* (Jeremiah 1:12, AMP). Waiting denotes entwining ourselves around the Lord as a vine entwines around a pillar and grows.

If ever there was a scripture for waiting on God's time for fulfilment, this is it:

For the vision is yet for an appointed time and it hastens to the end [fulfillment]; it will not deceive or disappoint. Though it tarry, wait [earnestly] for it, because it will surely come; it will not be behindhand on its appointed day.

Habakkuk 2:3 (AMP)

As You Wait...

The Lord is my portion..., says my living being (my inner self); therefore will I hope in Him and wait expectantly for Him.

Lamentations 3:24 (AMP)

What to do while you are waiting:

- Fill the well with the Word of God. Waiting on God's time reveals our heart of impatience. God's time is different than ours. *"But when the proper time had fully come, God sent His son."* (Galatians 4:4, AMP)
- Learn to wait in peace with no anxiety. This is a weapon of war. God is never anxious or stressed. The devil keeps us rushed and busy – hates our patience.
- Having done all, stand (Ephesians 6:13), but do all first. "Doing all" with regards your prophetic word is to agree with what God says, write it out and pray through all the areas mentioned. War over your word. Trust God to bring it to pass. It is *"faith and patience"* (Hebrews 6:12, NIV) that inherits the promises.

If you are called you will be sent, and if you are sent you will go. God makes the mission impossible for you to do so that you *must* lean on Him to do it through you. That is the point.

The Lord God is my strength, my personal bravery and my invincible army. He makes my feet like hind's feet, and will make me to walk and to make progress upon my high places of [trouble, suffering or responsibility].

Habakkuk 3:19 (AMP)

How long do I wait? Probably until you can say as in James 1:4, *"[I am letting] endurance and steadfastness and patience have full play and do a thorough work so that [I] may be perfectly and fully developed ... lacking in nothing."*

CHAPTER SIX

Personal Prophecy

This chapter addresses the how, what, when, where and the why of prophecy.

The Greek word "propheteuo" means "to foretell events, speak under inspiration" (i.e. "to prophesy").

So, How Do I Become Prophetic?

To prophesy literally means "to pour forth, to gush out" like a river.

The closer we stay to the Lord the more prophetic we become (if you believe that the definition of "being prophetic" is simply about hearing God). In Acts 19:6, as Paul laid hands on the believers to be baptized in the Holy Spirit, they also prophesied. *All* may prophesy, but many choose not to. It is part of the package that is Christ in us, the hope of glory. It is a gift of, and from, the Holy Spirit, and God loves to speak through us to other people and situations.

Prophets are geared and wired and equipped to get you from where you are now into where God wants you to be. They will bring you from your wilderness and into your Promised Land. Their calling encompasses changing the status quo of normalcy as we know it into something in God that is outside our theological concepts thus far.

What is prophecy? Revelation 19:10 says it is *"...the substance ... of the truth revealed by Jesus"* (AMP).

How we present and portray Jesus, through prophecy, is crucial; therefore we must steep our brains in everything that demonstrates the way He thinks and is. And He is the Word of God.

Personal prophecy is to draw out of a person what God has put in (e.g. Jesus prophesies over Peter and calls him "Peter the Rock"). God calls Gideon out of his hiding place where he is depressed and fearful and declares to him his destiny, calling him a "mighty man of valour". God always sees our potential and then allows us to see it as well. There are many selah moments.

Prophecy is about God revealing His will, thoughts and intentions to a group, person, situation or region. I believe that the greater role of a prophet is to teach, train and equip people to hear from God themselves.

One of the main roles of prophetic office is to point people to God to find out what His nature is and how He thinks. We could spend our entire lives simply abandoned to that purpose. We need a good understanding of the nature and character of God, and to be healed of our own wounds, particularly those sustained in the Father's house, to effectively and in truth bring the personal prophetic word. The way in which we portray God to a person, particularly His Father's heart, can either edify or discourage. Prophets and prophetic people, particularly, continually come from God's Father-heart of encouragement. This is our integrity. As prophets, we are "body builders" rather than merely blessing carriers.

> A word fitly spoken in season is like apples of gold in settings of silver.
>
> *Proverbs 25:11 (ESV)*

How?

We are drawn by our passion as prophetic people, and without a vision we fare badly.

Ask yourself these questions: "What am I seeing?" "What am I sensing?" "What am I hearing?" "What am I knowing?" "What am I painting?" "What am I writing?" "What am I composing?" "What am I singing?" "How does the Lord want me to express Him through my prophetic gifting?" "What is my goal in the prophetic?"

"What are the weaknesses in me or in my gifting?" "When am I crippled with fear, shame and/or rejection?"

God is always looking for the "broken and contrite heart" within us – in other words, the development of His character in us.

I have the confidence and faith that if I ask God for a prophetic word, that's exactly what He will give me. Luke 11:11 says, *"If a son shall ask bread of any of you that is a father, will he give him a stone?"* (KJV) A rhetorical question. Answer: Of course not!

If I ask the question, God will answer. He says, *"Call unto Me and I will answer you and show you great and mighty things that you do not know..."* (Jeremiah 33:3, NIV). This does not necessarily mean we will hear what we want. He may say, "Yes," "No," or "Wait."

We develop the gift, and as we prophesy more the gifting is developed.

As our identity in God is made more secure and our intimacy with Him is healed, we find that guidance always follows intimacy. As we are reconciled to God and then reconciled to our own selves, we are then more adequately equipped to reconcile with others. We often don't hear God because of a breakdown in our communication (ours, not His). In our natural lives, intimacy can produce conception. So it is in the spirit. There are many quiet, hidden "births in stables" as the wing of God overshadows what He wants to reproduce in us. Remember, our spirit-man is already hearing and seeing heaven as we are *"seated ... with Him in the heavenly realms in Christ Jesus"* (Ephesians 2:6, NIV). As we quieten down and listen, we will hear. It's about learning to live from our spirit rather than our soul. Our soul can be way too fat.

Rest is about letting the peace of God reign. He is the Prince of peace and He lives in us by His Spirit. Every place we are healed and restored in, we can have an authority in.

When?

When we prophesy over a person, we can ask God for different concepts of a person's life. Ask the Lord, "What would You like to say about this person's emotions, calling, finances, family, concerns, relationships, mission, travel, health, etc.?"

Ask, "Does the Lord want to give a word from His Word, a picture, a parable, a proverb, a movie title, a song, a road sign, etc.?" God can use anything to bring His essence into a person's life.

Critique your gift by asking your mentor to share what they observe. Be prepared for scrutiny, but remember, it's always to be given through love. Dare to submit to someone who just might know more and be a few toenails ahead of you. Ask yourself, "Where does God want to go in this?" and, "How do I get there?"

Learn from watching others. Be mentored, if possible, by someone who adores Jesus and wants to draw the best out of you. Serve that person and stick close to them, like Elisha and Elijah.

Constantly visualize. Write emails. Send cards. Believe that if someone else can prophesy with deep revelation, so can you. Practice being specific without waffling and repetition. Practice. Practice. Practice. Prophesy every day, every pray. Expect to hear clearly from the Lord when you are in prayer. He loves to express Himself to us.

We know we prophesy in part (1 Corinthians 13:9) as God shows us what we need for now. Prophecy is always partial, progressive and conditional. There will always be many "ifs" and "buts" which may or may not be mentioned. That is the conditional part.

We may know of ministry coming but not be told of all the P.I.T. stops (e.g. David, Joseph and Abraham).

God always speaks to potential; Gideon in Judges 6:12 and Ezekiel in Ezekiel 37. It will often be more about what God wants to say rather than what you want to hear.

Ask yourself with regards to the prophetic words you have received, "What is the overall message?" "Do they mention training I will need?" "How do they relate to my gifts and my talents?"

"What is my responsibility to fulfil this word now?" "Is it for now or in the future?" "Is there a thread running through all of these words over the years?"

Remember also that the voice of God in a prophetic word will always be consistent with His character and bring a sense of knowing and peace to your spirit. There will often be words and pictures, even parables and proverbs. There may be unusual content and something you may not have heard suggested before.

Often it is the time between the calling and the commissioning for that call, that we can lose the plot. This is what I call the bridge, and it is made of trust.

Revelation 19:10 says, *"...the substance ... of the truth revealed by Jesus is the spirit of all prophecy..."* (AMP). It is vital that we have a testimony of Jesus that is true and displays His character, His mercy, His goodness and His love, rather than our bitterness, our pain and our judgement, based on our history and unhealed wounds.

Our testimony is about who Jesus is to me now at this present moment. My history is about how I came to arrive at this place. My first love towards Jesus is the love of a rescued drowning person toward my rescuer. I am eternally grateful and now have life instead of slow death.

My love deepens as I get to know and love this incredible King who could actually be bothered with me in all my frailty.

But what if I've Missed It?

Don't be so obsessed with being accurate that you miss the intent and purpose of God to a person. There can be a perfectionist, religious spirit in the church that says you are a false prophet if you miss it. Religion is always about performance and being right. It has to die. God has perfect ways to set up that execution.

Intimidation, fear of man, fear of failure, our wounds and character issues keep us from achieving greatness in God more than anything else. Like learning to swim, we must get in the water to practice. Spend good quality time with strong prophetic people who are sold out to Jesus and to relationship and community; people who will nurture you through the process, be honest, but also show you grace. Find where you can fit and belong in a Christian community, where you can be built up in friendships and be loved and mentored well.

Whatever you speak to in the person will respond. We look for the gold in the dirt, not the dirt itself. I describe myself as a gold prospector, a word processor. We look at the treasure not the earthen vessel, separate the precious from the vile, and speak to the Christ in the person, the musician, the writer, the shepherd, and the destiny and the potential. We draw out what God has planted and unroll the hitherto sealed orders. We also deposit some new truth too.

God wants to put His words in our mouth, not ours in His.

We can make a quality decision to trust God that if we ask for a prophetic word that is edifying, uplifting and encouraging, He will give it.

Just as the mailman is not responsible for explaining what your letter says, or how to pay the bill he has just delivered, so the prophetic word has to simply be given. As a prophet you are not responsible for how that word will be unpacked or discerned. Don't shoot the messenger.

> The one who prophesies speaks to men for their upbuilding and constructive spiritual progress and encouragement and consolation.
>
> *1 Corinthians 14:3 (AMP)*

We need to use plenty of "if", "but", "I feel", "I sense" rather than the irrevocable "God says" or the religious "thus saith the Lord".

Prophesy "every day, every pray". 1 Corinthians 14:31 says, *"For you can all prophesy in turn, so that everyone may be instructed and encouraged."* (NIV)

God judges success by our faithfulness to do what He has asked. We need to develop consistency in being faithful and obedient.

Personal Prophecy

Paul says in 1 Corinthians 14:39, *"...earnestly desire and set your hearts on prophesying."* (AMP) In verse 5, same chapter he expresses his desire that, *"I want you to prophesy ... he who prophesies ... is ... more useful ... than he who speaks in ... tongues."* (AMP). Absolutely!

In 1 Thessalonians 5:19 Paul talks about quenching the Holy Spirit and in verse 20 he speaks of not depreciating prophetic revelations but also the importance of testing everything.

Testing Prophecy

One of the truest indications that a word is from the Lord and inspired by the Holy Spirit is your own response in your spirit.

Peace will always accompany a word from God, even if it is a challenging one. Your spirit agrees and says a large YES to the word.

There will never be any shame attached to a word from God, who knows that all our past sins are covered by His love at the Cross. Even if the Lord makes us uncomfortable by his goading and prodding, we should still feel loved and accepted, although challenged. I find God's discipline very gentle and loving. If He yelled at me I would simply die.

We should feel drawn to Him, never driven to performance but only drawn to grace. That's God.

It may be new truth that appears outside our realm of reference, but if we have a peace that it is still from the Holy Spirit we can examine it all later. The voice of God is always consistent and assuring, even when it is unusual. You can also run it by someone you trust and who loves you and, more importantly, does not despise prophecy.

Sometimes we tend to ask, "Is this me or God?" The short answer is, "It is both me *and* God." What a team! 1 Corinthians 13:9 says *"...our prophesy ... is fragmentary (incomplete and imperfect)."* (AMP) How true. Step out of the boat and start to swim in the waters.

A Few Guidelines and Protocols

When we are starting out in exercising our prophetic gift it is vital to have some protocols, ethics, and guidelines.

- Always ask permission of the person for whom you have a prophetic word, as not everyone wants one. It is very unusual for a person *not* to want one but it is simply manners to ask first.
- Some people are under the misapprehension that because you are prophetic you can see their entire life including what they had for breakfast. That is why more teaching on prophecy is essential.
- Ask if you may touch them, hold their hand etc. Ask the person's name and affirm them in prayer from the start and at the end. People need to feel safe and loved.
- *Never* embarrass or shame a person. We all have enough brokenness being healed as it is.
- God may "speak" through a "logos" word, a "rhema" word, a song, a picture, a sense, a prophetic action, a diagnostic word of knowledge, or a word of wisdom. If you ask for a thought, sensing-word, or picture from God, then you will receive it – having cast down stupid, vain imaginings and bound every demonic spirit of fear and lies, and centred yourself in God – so simply give the word. On the one hand, don't be apologetic, but on the other don't be a grandstanding celebrity either. Everyone looks more attractive when moving in the anointing of God and it is important to be aware that we do not seek the praises of man but only to please God.
- Stay within the realms of comfort, edification, encouragement (1 Corinthians 14:3) except for seasoned, mature prophets who may direct, correct and rebuke. All in the love of God of course.
- Keep using your gifting; pray and prophesy constantly.

- Don't be afraid to prophesy into a wider range than you are comfortable with such as finances, emotions, family, physical, ministry etc.

- Stir up the gift! Dig deep each time; fill your own "well" with the Word of God so it is fresh.

- Practise "listening prayer"; practise being quiet before God, listening to His voice. When He speaks it is like a single drop of water in a shady pool of silence. Train yourself to listen.

- Meditate on His Word; fill the well daily. Learn to wait on God frequently. Waiting on God is about being quiet and still, and waiting with a purpose.

- Learn to move out on the smallest hint of an impression; wade out into the deep.

- If you get a word of knowledge, use it! Then pray release to the person or place or situation that it is for.

- Use clear, modern day English, do not use "Christianese". (No "lo, beholdest, thouest sayest unto us-eth, the brethren" etc. I think you get the message.) Give the word and don't embellish, explain or repeat unnecessarily the same words. Jesus isn't particularly "wordy", is He? It's usually a couple of gentle words that speak volumes to us. Just be yourself in God, relatable to the culture.

- Believe God can speak into the person's life, situation or problem. We are merely the vehicle of conveyance.

How to Hear More Clearly

Here are some guidelines of how to hear more clearly:

- Realize that the prophetic word comes from our spirit not our mind. It is a prophetic revelation from the Spirit of God to our spirit.

- We must cultivate peace and rest because when we are prophesying there will always be a battle between the soul and the spirit for ascendancy.

- Listen to your heart; you will hear God. Begin to trust that.
- Practise rest; don't allow the devil to steal your peace under any circumstances. Practise the presence of Jesus.
- Learn not to react to your circumstances; choose your response carefully.
- Know your position is above, seated in heavenly places, not underneath them.
- Be quick to hear, slow to speak.
- Have quiet confidence. Isaiah 30:15 is one of my favourite verses in the Bible. It says, *"In quietness and confidence shall be your strength."*
- Learn the ways of God, how He thinks, how He wars, how He heals, how He prays, how He speaks etc..

When we are in the wilderness and long dark soul nights, we desperately want a prophet. When things are going great, we usually don't. But prophets are able to bring you from one place to another, from outside to in.

Sheep know the voice of their Shepherd. The more we hear His voice, the more we recognize it as Him. Those nearest and dearest to us are easily recognized through times spent together. The enemy's voice is usually driving and controlling, and has no sense of love in it. It will suggest self-justification, self-defence and protection of the flesh. It simply does not sound the same as the Lord's voice.

Wait, There's More!

- Feed on the Word of God. Understand how God thinks. Knowing the Word is no substitute for knowing God, though. It is like getting married and never speaking. We need both.
- Know guidance from the Holy Spirit. The Bible is the map to the Kingdom. The Kingdom is righteousness, peace and joy.
- Hear from other Christians with prophetic words or songs.

- Dreams, visions, prophetic acts, road signs, billboards, movies, book titles etc. are all valid ways to hear God speak or see something he is showing. He likes to get our attention. He is not confined to any box we may want to put Him in.

Solitude, not Isolation

Pressure often kills off those who are young in the prophetic. We need to stay in revelation and not come into reason and logic, or we can lose sight of God in a situation. We can find ourselves in isolation for a variety of reasons. Isolation is a breeding ground for deception and error. When others persecute us and we isolate, the answer, as hard as it is, is to seek fellowship in community. As I mentioned earlier, we are wounded in relationships but, conversely, we are healed in relationships.

If we operate from fear, anger and unhealed wounds, we will still hear messages but they will be polluted ones coming through our filter of bitterness. Taking time-out for healing causes us to face our fear of obscurity, which is often a big deal to prophets and those who seek to be seen and heard. Suspicion leads to delusion, and many aspiring prophets have lost it here. Don't let isolation into your heart. It is a lo-o-o-o-o-o-o-ong road back.

The Progression

I believe God can speak to this person
↓
I believe He can speak through me to this person
↓
I step into the mind of Christ (1 Corinthians 2:16) through my own mind
↓
I step into the prophetic anointing and prophesy

The Voice

We need stop listening to other voices, including our own. You need to be still and listen to your heart. You will hear God. Watch for the sensings, nudgings, faint images, and then step out. The sheep that stay close recognize His voice.

Hindrances to Prophesying

If we have too much busyness, frenzied human activity and distraction, it will cause us to lose our peace. In Colossians 3:15 we are encouraged to *"let the peace ... (which comes) from Christ rule ... in [our] hearts"* (AMP). Prophets need a lot of time alone in the solitude of the Holy Spirit, loving Him and listening. We need to be firm about this.

Bitter root judgement towards parents, those in authority and others in our lives can cause us to perpetuate the same type of wounding in our own lives. Often we become like the one we judge.

Fear and timidity, intimidation and having your voice shut down over the years, and creating an emotional autism, can stop us from releasing the word of the Lord.

Unhealed Wounds

Offence will blind us to truth. God offends the mind to reveal the heart. Until we address our rejection, our trauma, our fears, our abuse, our anger and our grief we may prophesy through them and wound others.

Biblical Examples of Where the Prophet Seemed to "Miss It"

There are times in the Bible where the prophet seemed to miss it by a country mile:

- Jonah prophesied that Nineveh would be overthrown in forty days, and the Lord changed His mind because the people repented.
- Isaiah had to retract a prophecy when a King prayed and asked God to spare his life.
- Agabus (Acts 21:27-33) prophesied that the Jews would bind Paul up, but it was actually the Gentiles.

It is only a religious, judgemental voice that says there is no room for failure; it is not God's voice. The Father is full of grace and mercy and is the God of a million chances, not just the second chance.

Fear will prevent us from giving out, and cause us to compromise the word of God.

Where?

The "logos" is all scripture within the Bible. There are two forms: the written word; and the *"word made flesh"*, who is Jesus. The Bible gives us general guidelines and principles to live by and wisdom to choose right from wrong, but not between two right things.

The "rhema" originates from God. It is a "Holy Spirit-inspired" word bringing life and power, and faith to perform it. It will be a personal revelation to the one receiving the word.

When we first begin in this area of personal prophecy we can start by being guided by specific areas, such as family, finances, physical, emotions and ministry.

The Difference between "Logos" and "Rhema"

"LOGOS" IS LIKE:	"RHEMA" IS LIKE:
The word in the Bible	A word from the Word
The wisdom of God	A word of wisdom
The knowledge of God	A word of knowledge
The well of the Word	A bucket from the well

We aim to touch every area in a person to liberate, heal, activate and release.

More Hows

- We do not go beyond our anointing. Do not go beyond your faith level. We do not add to or subtract from what God gives us nor do we need to explain ourselves.
- Like electricity we need to be plugged in to the right power source and know where the switch is to turn on and off. Try not to waffle or repeat the same thing several times. Stop when God stops. This is when less is more.
- Call your spirit man to life, to attention. Learn how to step into the anointing. Let God flow through you. Begin to prophesy; move from your spirit not your mind. Having cast down vain imaginings and bound the demonic realm in the situation, prophesy!
- Pray in tongues to allow your spirit to soar over your mind. Paul prayed in tongues more than the whole Corinthian church, and he moved powerfully in the spiritual giftings.

Prophecy can be Partial, Progressive and Conditional

PARTIAL:

The partial nature of prophecy is a comfort and a caution. Because God does not mention an area that the "logos" word is directing you to, it is not because He overlooks it (e.g. Moses and his uncircumcised son in Exodus 4:23).

PROGRESSIVE:

Paul was called as a light to the Gentiles. He did not know the whole story, nor what his journey would be. Joseph was not told of the pits on the way to the throne, only that he would rule.

John the Baptist was told that he was to prepare the way of the Lord and make His paths straight, but never told about his early death.

Abraham's life was a series of prophetic guidance, starting at age fifty. He was guided through his entire life as faith was built and promises fulfilled. It is *"faith and patience"* that inherits the promises.

CONDITIONAL:

Prophecy can be conditional whether the conditions are mentioned or not. They can be cancelled, reduced or diminished (e.g. God brought the Israelites into Canaan the Promised Land and ultimately unbelief shut them out). Out of one and a half million Israelites, only two people, Joshua and Caleb had the faith to believe they could all enter (Hebrews 4:2). In Numbers 13:30 we read how the dream was lost to the majority of the people, when Joshua and Caleb encouraged them not to fear and not to rebel; the people wanted to stone them.

Disobedience and Unbelief can Negate Prophecy

When God says, "I will," He means, " *We* will, together, if you will remains subject to My will."

God prophesies potential, like putting a bucket in the well into the water between the dregs at the bottom and the shallowness at the top.

Like a muscle, as long as you keep using the gift it will remain activated. Continually read, go to prophetic seminars, hang with prophetic people, keep praying and prophesying.

Some ways to ensure we do not negate prophecy:

- Remember that some areas to prophesy into are stronger in us than others (e.g. finances, emotions, ministry and callings, music, business, weather, politics).
- Practice all the five senses in the spirit.
- Critique your gift. Find a mentor, obviously not one who despises prophecy. Find accountability, particularly if you begin public ministry exploits.

- Covet to prophesy; be very determined, force yourself to go deeper and visualize constantly.
- The spirit of the prophet is subject to the prophet (1 Corinthians 14:32). We can hold on to a prophetic word until the right time in God. We really don't have to "burst forth" until God allows.
- Use the idiom of the day; we no longer live in the days of King James and it is only our strong religiosity that causes us to believe we are more valid and God inspired if we "thee and thou" and "lo and hereunto" everybody. Simply speak as you would to a friend, in fact as Jesus speaks to you.

Fallacies and Myths

1. "Seek the giver not the gift." We need to seek both, but *"...seek first His kingdom and His righteousness, and all these things will be given to you as well."* (Matthew 6:33, NIV). We need to seek His hand and, more importantly, His face. Paul, who exercised the spiritual gifts more than the whole Corinthian church, exhorts us to *"...earnestly desire and set your hearts on prophesying (on being inspired to preach and teach and to interpret God's will and purpose), and do not forbid or hinder speaking in ... tongues"* (1 Corinthians 14:39, AMP).

2. In Numbers 11:27, a young man dashed up to Moses to complain that Eldad and Medad were prophesying in the camp. Moses replied saying, *"Are you jealous for my sake? I wish that all the Lord's people were prophets and the Lord would put His spirit on them."* (Verse 29, NIV). Absolutely!

3. "I got it wrong, I am a false prophet." No, not false, but maybe untried and immature in the gifting. Any voice that says there is no room for failure is not from God. We will succeed with God when we are willing to fail in front of our peers. God is loaded with grace for our many shortcomings.

4. One of the signs of a false prophet is one who draws people to himself rather than points them to God; one who prophesies from the soul, manipulating and controlling through prophecy; or one who wants to be a spiritual "guru" to a person.

5. "I have grieved the Holy Spirit." Maybe, but He is probably used to it and is bigger than our messes. God's grace is ever towards us when we make a mistake. Stay accountable to a mature, seasoned prophet who will help you through the maze. Be prepared to fall and fail and look a fool sometimes. Sometimes insecure people hate teams. They cannot face being wrong. Allow God to plant you in a team that encourages and wants everyone to do well. Part of dying to your own selfish ambition is asking God to develop in you a desire to see other team members do better than you, to go further. Recognize control and manipulation in yourself and shoot it. Defer to others and prefer others in love. We all build on someone else's shoulders. Allow yours to be used.

Failing does not make you a failure; it is simply an opportunity to try again. Our success in God will always be about our faithful hearts.

For though a righteous man falls seven times, he rises again.

Proverbs 24:16 (NIV)

Learning to move in your prophetic gifting is like learning to navigate a large ship through a dangerous reef, but the rewards in God are worth it all.

The Lord is a majestic king and a wonderful Father who understands our desire to be involved in a great adventure, an exciting quest. Kingdom living is the only way to live to please the King.

Prophetic words are powerful and nurturing and can change the course of a person's life for good. Many times people have said to me, even years later, that the prophetic word they received sustained them throughout a life crisis, or that it had all come out as the word had said and had directed their path in a life-giving way.

Be encouraged. Venture out. You are called to be a blessing and a joy to many people.

CHAPTER SEVEN

Types of Prophecy

There are a number of different types of prophecy:

- Biblical
- Messianic
- Personal
- Partial
- Progressive
- Conditional
- Unconditional
- Revelatory
- Inspirational
- Eschatological ("End-time")

Biblical

If prophecy is defined as God communicating with man, then the Bible is an entire prophetic word spoken by God to man in written form.

> Every scripture is God breathed (given by His inspiration) and profitable for instruction, for reproof and conviction of sin, for correction of error and discipline in obedience and for training in righteousness.
>
> *2 Timothy 3:16 (AMP)*

Messianic

Messianic prophecies are prophecies pertaining to Christ's first and second coming (Micah 5:2, Isaiah 53).

David prophesied an eternal heir to the throne in the Psalms. Isaiah spoke of the suffering servant of mankind. Daniel prophesied the victorious coming of Jesus the King. Each was a partial revelation of the whole counsel of God. It all points to Jesus – His birth, life, death, resurrection and second coming.

Personal

Personal prophecy is God revealing his personal thoughts and intentions to a person(s), group, place, and/or situation.

Why do we need it? The Bible gives us general guidelines and principles to live by, because it is the "logos", written, inspired Word, but not the daily guidance pertaining to the decisions of life.

John is the first to use the term "logos" pertaining to Jesus. He stated Jesus *is* the Word. (1 John 1:1, 5:7; John 1:1, 1:14). In Revelation 19:13 we read that He has a title: the Word of God.

The "logos" will only be effective as we apply it to our lives by an act of our will coupled with faith. It is the standard by which mankind and the whole of creation is judged. All revelation and doctrine must line up with the "logos". In Proverbs 16:11 we read, *"A just balance and scales are the Lord's: all the weights of the bag are His work..."* (AMP)

The "logos" judges everything including prophecy. It evaluates other belief systems, doctrines, ministries etc.

> Anyone who rejects Me and sets Me at naught has his judge for the very message that I have spoken will judge and convict him at the last day.
>
> *John 12:48 (AMP)*

(Further scriptures on this topic are found in Revelation 20:12, John 1:8, and James 2:12.)

So, personal prophecy is a Holy Spirit inspired word that brings life and dynamic revelation and the power to perform it. It should agree with the weight of scripture and also the spirit of it. (For example, a prophet may give a prophetic word that is in agreement with the weight and heart of "logos", but if the person bringing the word is harsh and judgemental, this is not the spirit of Christ.)

Biblical examples of personal prophecy:

- God spoke to Adam about what his role in the Garden of Eden was and how to have dominion over the earth (Genesis 1,2,3).
- God spoke to Noah about building an ark to preserve life – exact proportions and dimensions – and how to rescue the animals (Genesis 6:14-22).
- God progressively prophesied to Abraham about moving to Canaan, the promised son Isaac and his ministry to the world (Genesis 12:24).
- Jacob prophesied to his sons about being the twelve tribes of Israel (Genesis 49).
- Joshua was told by God how to win the city of Jericho (Joshua 6:2-5).
- Samuel prophesied to Saul about his lost donkeys and that he was to be the first king of Israel (1 Samuel 9:19).
- An angel prophesied to Mary about her being the mother of Jesus, gave her his name and told of His future ministry (Luke 1).
- Jesus spoke to Peter about his personality, mistakes, ministry and mode of death.
- Jesus in his resurrected body appeared and spoke to Paul (Acts 9).
- Ananias laid hands on Paul, prophesied his ministry, released healing and the gift of the Holy Spirit (Acts 9).
- Prophets and prophetic presbytery prophesied Paul and Silas's appointment to apostolic itinerant ministry.

- Paul and the Presbytery team laid hands on Timothy, releasing him to ministry.

Remember, you do not need to understand or explain the word you give; you are simply the vehicle, the deliverer of the word, the messenger.

These are words from the Bible that were for a particular situation only:

- Throw a stick in the water and the iron will float to the top (2 Kings 6:6).
- Throw meat into a poisoned pot of food to make it nutritious (2 Kings 4:41).
- Sort out your finances by filling many barrels with oil from one small bottle (2 Kings 4:2).
- Point a rod towards the sea and it will open before you and you will run across to the other side (Exodus 15:25).
- Spit on blind eyes to heal them (Mark 8:23).
- March around the walls of a city and they will fall down (Joshua 6).

These were some of the acts prophets were asked to do, for a specific purpose only:

- Ezekiel was told by God to lie on his left side for three hundred and ninety days and then on his right side for forty days to bear the iniquity of the ten tribes of Israel (Ezekiel 4:4).
- Isaiah had to walk barefoot and naked for three years as a sign concerning Egypt and Ethiopia (Isaiah 20:3).
- Hosea had to marry a prostitute and have children with her as a prophetic demonstration of what Israel was doing in her relationship to God (Hosea 1:2).
- Ezekiel had to shave his head and beard and divide the hair into three parts (Ezekiel 5).

- Elisha's commissioning in 1 Kings 19 instructed him to "burn his plough". Sometimes, however, God will challenge us to give up a well-paid job to follow Him into a ministry role.

(The personal prophecy of God to a person does not establish doctrine or Christian practice. Sadly, many cults are formed this way.)

Partial

Prophecy will sometimes be more about what God wants to say than what you want to hear. Paul says in 1 Corinthians 13:9, *"For we know in part and we prophesy in part."* (NIV)

Many times we may be told what our ministry is that we are called to but not have the whole plan of the journey. We may be shown the purpose without the plan. If we knew by what means God would equip us and build His character in us we may never choose to go!

Examples of partial prophecy:

- Moses – called by God to deliver Israel from Egypt. He was not initially told of the process by which it would happen.
- Joseph – called by God to be mighty ruler. He was not told of the pit stops on the way to the throne.
- David – called as a King over Israel. He was not told of the process.
- Paul – God spoke to Ananias that Paul was called to the Gentiles and to the Jews (Acts 9) and that he was to lay hands on him to heal his temporary blindness, but God also said to Ananias, *"I will make clear to him how much he is to be afflicted and must endure and suffer for my name's sake."* Paul found out the plan "on the way", as we all do.
- Abraham – was told by God he would become *"a great nation"* but not how it would come about.

God says in Deuteronomy 29:29, *"The secret things belong to the Lord our God, but the things revealed belong to us and our children forever..."* (AMP)

Progressive

Prophecy can build *"line upon line, precept upon precept"* (Isaiah 28:13). We might be overwhelmed if God gave us the full picture immediately.

The outcome of the "progressive" is the "suddenly", and like a pregnancy, suddenly there is a birthing of something conceived in the heart of God and kept until the appointed time. If we rush on before God is ready we will produce something of our own carnality rather than of the spirit (e.g. Ishmael and Isaac).

Some Biblical "suddenly"s following the progressive word:

- Noah progressively prepared and worked for years without evidence from God when *suddenly* it began to rain.
- Moses had the supernatural manifestations and the commissioning with power. He had two years of going before Pharaoh who ultimately hardened his heart towards Moses, but *suddenly* God moved and they left for the Promised Land.
- David, as a teenager received a prophetic word from Samuel declaring his coming kingship. It took seventeen years from a shepherd, who had to then kill a lion and a bear, and killed Goliath, to becoming captain of one thousand, then *suddenly* King of Israel.

Abraham is a classic progressive prophecy leading to ultimate fulfilment. At age fifty (Genesis 12:1) Abraham was sent to Haran. At age seventy-five, God prophesies that Abram will become a great nation and says in Genesis 12:2, *"...and I will make your name famous and distinguished and you will be a blessing [dispensing good to others]."* (AMP) On arrival in Canaan, God continues to prophesy that this is the land He will hand on to his descendants.

In Genesis 13 we read that Lot chooses Sodom and God prophesies to Abram that He will make his descendants as many as *"the dust of the earth"* (verse 16, AMP). In Genesis 15 the details of the bigger plan are revealed: that his descendants will be as many as the stars; that his people will be held in captivity for four hundred years but eventually brought out to freedom; and that the fourth generation will possess the land. God makes a covenant with Abraham over the land.

At age ninety-nine (Genesis 17), God appears to him and exhorts him to *"...walk and live habitually before [him] and be perfect (blameless, wholehearted, complete)"* (AMP). He is given a new name: from Abram ("high exalted father") to Abraham ("the father of a multitude"). He is also given a new covenant (circumcision) and the promise of the son Isaac (twenty-four years after the original prophecy). When Abraham is a hundred years old, Isaac is born. In the same year God pronounces judgement on Sodom and Gomorrah.

Abraham's entire life was a demonstration of personal progressive prophecy. The plan for our whole life is revealed partially and progressively with conditions.

Abraham and Sarah waited twenty-five years for the fulfilment of Isaac. David waited about twenty years for the fulfilment of his kingship. Joseph waited twenty-two years for the outworking of his word. Psalm 105:19 says *"...until his word [to his cruel brothers] came true, until the word of the Lord tried and tested him."* (AMP)

Conditional

In Exodus 6:5-8 it is prophesied about the Israelites leaving Egyptian bondage and coming into freedom. Out of six hundred thousand adult men only two, Joshua and Caleb, embraced the prophetic word and walked into it. The Word did not fail, but because of doubt and unbelief, 599,998 failed to walk into their inheritance. Moses prophesied the Word in Exodus 6:5-8. He was not a false prophet, but the word found no root in the hearers. It is the same today. Remember, prophets are meant to bring you from your wilderness and into the land of your inheritance.

> ...neither were they united in faith with the ones [Joshua and Caleb] who heard (did believe).
>
> *Hebrews 4:2 (AMP)*

Unconditional

These are prophetic words that will not be recalled by God under any conditions; the dynamic of the unconditional prophetic word being that it will come to pass ultimately. They may be readjusted but never revoked.

> For I am the Lord; I will speak and the word that I shall speak shall be performed ... it shall no more be delayed or prolonged for in your days ... I will speak the word and will perform it, says the Lord.
>
> *Ezekiel 12:25 (AMP)*

Examples of unconditional prophecy:

- The second coming of Jesus.
- The destruction of the natural world.
- The bruising of the "serpent's head" came not through Eve directly, but through Mary.
- The destruction of Nineveh. Although the city repented and was saved temporarily, they turned back to their evil ways and were destroyed.

Sometimes a prophetic word is postponed as in 2 Kings 20:6, where King Hezekiah became ill but through the prophetic word of Isaiah he was given another fifteen years to live. Isaiah also had a word of knowledge to apply a poultice of figs to the King's abscess, which was about to probably turn into a systemized septicaemia and bring about his death.

Revelatory

Prophecy that brings revelation to the hearers, which can be directional or even correctional, is revelation prophecy and needs to be put through the ethic and protocol of the leadership of a church before it is brought before the congregation. (For example, Paul's greatest revelation to the churches was that the Gentiles could partake of salvation as well as the Jews. This was described as a "revealed mystery" in Ephesians 3:3,6. And his revelation that the church *is* the body of Christ in Ephesians 3.)

> ...you are a letter from Christ delivered by us not written with ink but with the Spirit of God, not on tablets of stone but on tablets of human hearts.
>
> *2 Corinthians 3:3 (NIV)*

Inspirational

This is prophecy that comes in times of prayer together, worship, praise times, and is encouraging and edifying. It is often where prophetic people begin to prophesy and is safe ground.

Eschatological

The whole book of Revelation is an end-time prophetic word. 1 Thessalonians 4:16 is another one, where Paul wrote, *"For the Lord Himself will descend from heaven..."* (AMP). In Mark 13 we find that most of this chapter prophesies the second coming of Jesus.

CHAPTER EIGHT

Types of Prophetic Ministry

God has a certain order of authority within the church so that when everyone is able to identify their calling the whole "structure" can be built well.

> So God has appointed some in the church [for His own use]: first apostles ... second prophets ... third teachers, then wonder workers; then those with the ability to heal the sick; helpers; administrators; [speakers in] different ... tongues.
>
> *1 Corinthians 12:28 (AMP)*

God speaks to us in many and varied ways, and the various ways of expressing God prophetically are as diverse and imaginative as God wants to be. Here are some examples:

- The office of prophet
- The gift of prophecy
- Prophetic presbytery
- Prophetic preaching
- The spirit of prophecy
- Prophetic singing
- The arts (music, drama etc.)

Jesus was all the five-fold gifts embodied in Himself:

- The Apostle   Hebrews 3:1
- The Prophet   Acts 3:22-23
- The Evangelist   Matthew 9:35, Luke 4:18
- The Pastor   John 10:14, Hebrews 13:20, 1 Peter 2:25
- The Teacher   John 3:2, Mark 1:22, John 7:14, John 6:45

The Office of Prophet

The prophets are God's friends. Right back in the Old Testament, the Lord says in 1 Chronicles 16:22, *"...do My prophets no harm."* (AMP)

Ephesians 2:20 speaks of the church being built on the foundations of the apostle and prophet with Jesus as the chief cornerstone. So far we have seen the church built on the foundation of the pastor only, but this is now beginning to change as God's order brings alignment and God raises up apostles and prophets as the foundation. This is the transition that the church of the twenty-first century is going through, and whilst it looks chaotic at the moment, order will come as correct alignment is allowed.

Prophets are the "eyes", the seers of the body. It has become "normal" to have a church without prophets; however, without them the "body" will not have sufficient vision to move forward and will be partially blinded, particularly to the move of God in this present generation. We do need to be correctly related as a body to the head, Jesus. The closer we become to Jesus, the more we should be moving towards loving the body of Christ. You can't have one without the other.

When Jesus spoke revelatory and exposing truth to the people in the synagogue in Luke 4:18-32, initially they were delighted and spoke great accolades about Him. By the time He had finished, the Bible says (verse 28 onwards) that *"all the people in the synogogue were filled with rage"* (AMP), drove Him from the church and wanted to murder Him by hurling Him over a cliff! That was a very sparky sermon! Prophets will expose religiosity, hypocrisy and pretence, often just by being present.

In Luke 5, the Pharisees express distaste about the team Jesus is travelling with, pointing out that they are *"eating and drinking"* (verse 33, NIV). Oh what ghastly low people you hang with, Jesus! He never loses His cool, though; and, as usual, wins each time by answering a question with a question – a great ploy when confronted with judgemental religious critics, take note!

116

Surely the Sovereign LORD does nothing without revealing his plan to his servants the prophets.

Amos 3:7 (NIV)

The prophet stands expressing God to the people, the pastor represents the people before God, but the primary purpose of the prophet is to point *you* to hear God for yourself.

The Function of the Office of Prophet

- Provides direction (1 Kings 22:5,6,7,8; 2 Kings 5).
- Corrects (Ezekiel 3:18).
- Warns (1 Samuel 8:9,19).
- Pronounces judgement.
- Gives revelation knowledge (1 Samuel 9:19, Isaiah 44:24, 45:3, Daniel 10:1).
  As a prophet I sometimes say to my friends, with a smile of course, "Hello, let me tell you how you are!"
- Lays biblical foundations in church (Ephesians 2:20).
- Imparts spiritual gifts (Romans 1:11-12, 1 Timothy 4:14).
- Sets people in their ministry and anoints those ministries.
  Kings, priests and prophets were anointed by prophets into their ministries in the Old Testament:
  1. King Saul was anointed by Prophet Samuel (1 Samuel 10:1).
  2. The High priest Aaron was anointed by Prophet Moses (Exodus 28:41).
  3. Elijah the prophet anointed Elisha into his prophetic office (1 Kings 19:1).
  4. King David was ordained by Prophet Nathan (1 Samuel 16).
  5. King Solomon was ordained by Prophet Nathan.

The Gift of Prophecy

This is a gift given by Jesus, not an "office". It is for all believers everywhere. 1 Corinthians 14:31 says, *"For you can all prophesy in turn so that everyone may be instructed and encouraged."* (NIV) In other words, if you want, you may.

- It cannot be earned (1 Corinthians 4:7: *"What have you that was not given to you?"* AMP)
- It is to be simply received, like salvation (Ephesians 2:8).
- It cannot be purchased (Acts 8:18).
- It is operational immediately (Acts 19:6: *"And as Paul laid his hands upon them, the Holy Spirit came on them; and they spoke in (foreign, unknown) tongues (languages) and prophesied."*)
- We are encouraged to covet ("lust") after it as it has the potential to bless many (1 Corinthians 14:1, 14:39, 1 Corinthians 12:31).
- We are instructed to *"especially"* seek after prophesy because (1 Corinthians 14:5: *"...He who prophesies ... is ... (more useful ...) than he who speaks in ... tongues... ";* AMP)
- We are instructed to *"not treat prophecies with contempt"* (1 Thessalonians 5:20).

Prophecy, like the other giftings, is for the edification and encouragement of others (1 Peter 4:10). It was a normal occurrence in all the churches established by Paul; he revealed and released the Word of God through *revelation, knowledge, prophecy* and *doctrine,* and established churches throughout the known world based on this premise (1 Corinthians 14:6).

Prophetic Presbytery

Although it is a rather antiquated term, "presbytery" is a collection together of several elders or officers, including prophets and other five-fold ministers, managing the local church, as it was in the days of the early church. So a "prophetic presbytery" is a collection of prophets brought together for the purposes of four main functions:

- Prophetic revelation and confirmation of those called to leadership, as with Paul in the Antioch church separating those called to service (Acts 13:1-3).
- Ordination to five-fold ministry, done by five-fold ministers, including senior prophets. The prophet may reveal the call to a person, which is usually a confirmation of that call, but the ordination should come through prophetic presbytery. In Titus 1:5 Paul leaves Titus in charge of the new converts at Crete to *"...finish what was left undone, and ... appoint elders and set them over the churches... "* (AMP)
- The activation and confirmation of the believers into offices and ministries (Acts 6:3,6).
- Encouraging progressive maturity in the people. In Acts 14:22-23, a presbytery was formed that encouraged the people and ordained elders into ministry. In most instances hands were "laid on" to impart an anointing to do a certain thing. At Antioch, prophets *and* teachers were used in this capacity.

It is still a practised form of "setting apart" for the work of the ministry, bringing confirmation and godly endorsement.

Prophetic Preaching

My definition is, "Prophetic preaching is laying hold of the mind of God and preaching the words and actions from the heart of God for that precise moment to those particular people." It is a "now" word.

Preaching is about presenting biblical truths that have been researched and thoroughly studied. Most Bible colleges train people how to prepare sermons (homiletics) and how to deliver them (pulpit speech).

Although there is nothing wrong with that, prophetic preaching is the present truth for this moment in time, to these particular people.

It often brings revelation and breakthrough. The very word "prophetic" implies revelation knowledge and inspired words.

In prophetic preaching the "preacher" is not necessarily a prophet (although all prophets are well able to preach prophetically). Rather, the preacher is the carrier and courier of the message from the heart of God for that moment (i.e. present day truth in its deepest sense). It will be based on biblical truth and subject to the standard of the Word of God.

This is in essence "the Oracle of God" as Peter wrote in 1 Peter 4:11: *"Whoever speaks ... [let him do it as one who utters] oracles of God..."* (AMP), or, in other words, "speaks divine revelation".

The Spirit of Prophecy

> For it is the Spirit of prophecy who bears testimony to Jesus.
>
> *Revelation 19:10 (NIV)*

> For the substance of the truth revealed by Jesus is the spirit of all prophecy [the vital breath, the inspiration of all inspired preaching and interpretation of the divine will and purpose, including both mine and yours.]
>
> *Revelation 19:10 (AMP)*

This is about how we reveal and portray God to the people. This is different from both the "office" and the "gift".

My definition of the spirit of prophecy is, "The anointing arising from within the believer often occurring corporately across a congregation and particularly when other prophets are present and everyone finds it suddenly easy to prophesy." It may alight for a moment or a season then seem to leave again, like a wind of the Spirit.

It occurs particularly when:

- A company of prophets is present.
- The presence of Jesus *as prophet* comes and all begin to prophesy, just as at Pentecost "all spoke in tongues" because of the manifest presence of God.
- A prophet or prophetic minister or leader releases an anointing for "all to prophesy", and all do.

Biblical examples are:

- Zachariah begins to prophesy (Luke 1:63).
- Peter begins to prophesy (Acts 2:17).
- Pentecost (Acts 2).
- Messengers of Saul (1 Samuel 19:20-24).

Prophetic Singing

Jesus sings over us through prophets, psalmists and prophetic singers and musicians. This is the heart of God expressed through music and song, usually with words but not necessarily.

Any person may enter into the spirit of prophecy in song, but there will be a stronger anointing when the song comes through a prophet.

The "Song of the Lord" may be general to a group, a region, a nation or to an individual, as in personal prophecy. These are the minstrels of God to this generation.

Many times the Lord has led me to what I sense as "strategic spiritual locations" of headlands and coastlands in places in the world to simply prophesy to the land and worship Him there. I do not always know the reason but I do it anyway, and know something of Him is released there.

BIBLICAL EXAMPLES OF PROPHETIC SONG:

- Moses and the Israelites sang the song of the Lord (Exodus 15:1).

- *"...the women came ... singing and dancing."* (1 Samuel 18:6-7, AMP).

BIBLICAL EXHORTATION:

- *"Sing ... a new song..."* (Psalm 33:3, AMP)
- *"He has put a new song in my mouth..."* (Psalm 40:3, AMP)
- *"And they sang a new song..."* (Revelation 5:9, NIV)
- *"Speak out to one another in psalms and hymns and spiritual songs..."* (Ephesians 5:19, AMP)

(More information is given on this subject in chapter 14.)

The Arts, (Music, Drama etc.)

There is coming upon the church a new release of the restoration of all things creative as God is expressed yet again in all of the arts. We are seeing a restoration of art, music, drama and literature under the inspiration of the Holy Spirit. As we are put in touch with our creative selves so we are reconciled to the Creator God Himself as He is expressed through that creative self in the multiple and wonderful facets of the body of Christ.

Jesus longs to be expressed through us in all the creative forces of His own personality and particularly in times of worship and adoration of the true King of Creativity.

As with all created things, Satan has tried to distort and pervert that which was destined for the believers in Christ. Much has been stolen from us, but with the revelation of the Holy Spirit in prophetically activated creativity, it too is being restored to the church. Our postmodern theology needs to be demonstrated through not just words but through art, song, poetry, dance, sculpture etc.

In other indigenous cultures where singing, narration, art and dance are totally intrinsic to the culture, it would be perfectly normal to ask a wounded person, "When did you stop singing?" In our Western culture we have usually never started.

I see God building communities of artisans and poets, tribes joining with each other through common ideologies and relevant theologies. There will be healing communities, artists' communities, places of equipping and training in life skills, retreat houses, healing homes and prayer communities, and a whole new face on the existing model of what we call "church". Change is not only coming – it is here. Here and now. And thank God for it!

CHAPTER NINE

Ethics and Protocols of Prophecy

Ethics: "Moral principles, rules of conduct."

Protocol: "A standard of etiquette and personal behaviour."

Definitions from Oxford English Dictionary

Generally speaking, the ethics and protocol of personal prophecy, and in particular how to give one and receive one, have not been taught in churches sufficiently. We therefore have any number of "loose cannons" exploding everywhere, and not many to adequately disciple emerging prophets, and certainly not enough prophetic schools of credible value.

I was blessed to have been taught, trained and have mentoring by two or three excellent prophets in Australia. They were extremely releasing and well-grounded in the Word of God, with a passion for Jesus and an understanding of the personality and identity of prophetic people. I have hopefully carried that on to the many men and women I have personally mentored in the prophetic over the years. Time will tell.

The Lord sent me to England for seven years, where I was part of a fairly extensive prophetic community. We ran continual prophetic schools during the year as well as restoration healing schools. It is my personal opinion that the two streams need to run together, so that those being mentored in their gifting would also be on a heart journey of healing.

Many people are relocating geographically to where the Lord is pouring out His glory in a substantial way, and where they are able to finally be understood and raised up in their gifting.

Prophetic schools are not a modern idea. From the prophet Samuel right through to the end of the Old Testament, there was always a supply of prophets. In 1 Samuel 19:20 the story is told about *"the company of the prophets"* (AMP) with Samuel *"standing as appointed head over them"* (AMP). The prophetic anointing was so strong on this company that when King Saul came amongst them, seeking to kill David, the Holy Spirit fell on him too and he, even he, began to prophesy!

In 2 Kings 2 there is reference again to companies of prophets. In 2 Kings 6:1 there is a strong reference to the fact that there was a prophetic community which had gathered around Elisha and that there was not enough room for all of them, so they began to build a bigger house for them all.

Obadiah is also one of my heroes. He was a devout lover of God and during Jezebel's reign hid a hundred prophets in two caves (fifty in each), and kept them supplied with food and water. No mean task (1 Kings 18)!

First Priority

Humility and servanthood need to mark the life and ministry of all prophets and prophetic people and ministers. Jesus said, *"I am in your midst as One Who serves"* (Luke 22:27, AMP), and so must we be. The servant-heart attitude of Jesus is revealed in a number of Bible verses, including John 3:27, John 5:30, and John 8:28.

God seems to judge prophets and the prophetic gifting more quickly than any other.

This is mainly because of the enormity of the responsibility of being entrusted by Him to represent His character by speaking into the lives of His precious ones (those who know Him and those who don't). There is nothing like an accurate prophetic word, spoken in love, to reach the heart of a non-Christian and allow God to show Himself.

Submission and Faithfulness

Joshua submitted to Moses, Elisha submitted to Elijah, and the seventy elders submitted under Moses. As they submitted and served their leaders, the glory of God and the anointing of the leader came down on them like a mantle. We must be willing to wait on God for the timing of our release, and as we wait we serve those above us in authority and those around us in our life. Prophets have a long season of preparation as God builds His character in them, heals the broken places of the heart and develops patience.

As we wait on Him, we grow stronger in Him.

> Obey them that have the rule over you and submit to them.
>
> *Hebrews 13:17 (NIV)*

> Likewise ye younger submit to the elder. All of you be subject one to another and be clothed with humility: for God resists the proud and gives grace to the humble.
>
> *1 Peter 5:5 (KJV)*

Waiting on God for the release is usually part of our wilderness experience. The higher the calling, the deeper the foundation needs to be.

Faithfulness is about serving without recognition or acknowledgement. In every David there is some Saul, and in every Saul some David. Occasionally, God may put us through a time of serving Saul (that is, ungodly leadership), to test our hearts. It is part of the journey of ruling and reigning in our own lives.

Self-government is crucial to any other form of government. We need to develop faithfulness in matters of money, ministry, marriage, friendships and morality; in the little things and the big.

> Whoever can be trusted with very little can also be trusted with much, and whoever is dishonest with very little will also be dishonest with much ... And if you have not been trustworthy

with someone else's property, who will give you property of
your own?

Luke 16:10,12 (NIV)

False Prophets

I believe that a false prophet is one who continually draws people
to themselves for power, monetary gain, ambition, manipulation,
prestige, or recognition. It is one who wants to control, manipulate
and coerce through their gifting and works in the opposite spirit to
meekness and humility, which is the spirit of Jesus. The false prophet
wants to literally be the voice of God to you. If we did not have the
"real" we would never know the "counterfeit". A false prophet is
not a prophet who makes a mistake or misses it in the spirit. All five-
fold ministers make mistakes; it just so happens that prophets'
mistakes are far more public as a general rule.

The Bible talks about:

- False prophets (Matthew 23:11)
- False apostles (2 Corinthians 11:13)
- False teachers (2 Peter 2:1)
- False witnesses (Matthew 26:60)
- False brethren (Galatians 2:4)
- False Christs (Mark 13:22)

Accountability

I believe it is important as prophetic ministers to develop, where
possible, accountability and a mentoring relationship to God-
ordained authority. Ideally, of course, this is someone who totally
understands prophetic identity and how to nurture an emerging
prophet. When we release to God our need to control and
manipulate, our fear of obscurity and our craving for status, we can
begin to enter into accountability and service. Self-denial means I do
not have to insist on my own way, I do not need to be right all the

time and I do not have to control everybody. In other words, get over yourself.

When Invited to Minister

If we are invited to minister anywhere we must naturally observe ethics and protocol in the situation, find out what is required, how long, what are the boundaries, etc. Most importantly, find out who is in charge in any situation so you know whom to relate to from the very beginning. If we come with a servant heart we will usually be given more freedom in the spirit. We never criticize the facilities offered or their lack. Always make it clear in the beginning, if you are asked, what your requirements are, but do not be demanding or difficult. We are there to serve, not demand service.

We always operate in grace and always submit to leadership whether at the home-based church or away. We do not allow our gift to be prostituted but are always prepared to prophesy. There have been times in my own ministry, in the earlier years, when I was set up by people, asked to dinner or similar, to find a table full of people all expecting a personal prophecy. Many opportunities for grace!

You may want to buy a recording device, to be ready in season and out. It is wise protocol to record your words, if at all possible, to squash retaliation and twisting of words later.

Relax. There is always time in public prophetic ministry to inquire if words are being recorded by the sound engineer and, if not, organize a scribe to write at least the gist of what is about to be prophesied.

Respect those in authority over you and never presume to prophesy "upward" until you submit the word to someone in authority or eldership.

There has been more than enough freaky-cooky-craziness expressed in the name of the prophetic, and it is time now to act with decorum, order and genuine love, with no strings attached and no exhibitionism either.

Even Jesus asked, *"What do you want Me to do for you?"* Find out, if you are invited, what the expectation of the leader is before you go. I believe it is wise to inform those who invite you into churches that a Sunday morning ministry session delivered by a prophet is not going to solve twenty years of bad teaching and division, or whatever else the church is struggling with. Relationship will always be more important than gifting. Sometimes you may have an ongoing relationship with a group or church, to work alongside the leadership to bring adjustment and change, mediation and encouragement. Remember that the people can only go as far as the leadership will allow; to whatever level in God the leadership is, there will the people be also.

Dress modestly; people are watching so do not cause someone else to stumble because of your lack of sensitivity.

Even in your home church do not entertain "car park prophesying" like a sideshow entertainer.

Do not draw people to yourself, your ministry, your church, or your bank account; this is being a false prophet.

Never minister for prowess, prestige or monetary gain. This is not the heart of God.

> I urge you to live a life worthy of the calling you have received.
> Be completely humble and gentle; be patient, bearing with one
> another in love.
>
> *Ephesians 4:1-2 (NIV)*

The calling to prophetic ministry is a high calling, fraught with mishaps and misunderstandings, rejection and missed communication. It has enormous highs and miserable lows, but we are in it to serve the God of angel armies, to walk in humility and without offence. We all look brilliant under the anointing of Jesus, but never come into the adulation of people. We will always be trusted with more when we have demonstrated that we are trustworthy with the precious hearts of His people, and when we learn to carry the secrets of people and the secrets of God.

CHAPTER TEN

Ministering in the Gifts of the Spirit

Ideally, and biblically, five-fold ministers are called to equip the rest of the body (i.e. the church) for the work of doing the ministry of Jesus both within and without the church (Ephesians 4:12).

This is the precise reason that God has released some – note: *some* – to be apostles, prophets, teachers pastors or evangelists.

Things will happen when this is activated in a church:

- We begin to walk in oneness, in unity because we begin to actually understand who God really is.
- We grow up. We *"[arrive] at really mature manhood"* (Ephesians 4:13, AMP).
- We *"no longer"* act like *"children, tossed ... to and fro between chance gusts of teaching"* (Ephesians 4:14, AMP).
- We begin to express truth through love: *"speaking truly, dealing truly, living truly"* (Ephesians 4:15, AMP).

We need to stir up the gifts that are already resident and often dormant in us. What's the best gift? Answer: the one you need at the time.

God has freely bestowed gifts on us all. It is up to us to open them and use them. Don't deny people your gift. There are people and situations waiting for you to access your gift and use it!

These are the three areas of giftings in the Holy Spirit:

- The five-fold ministry gifts (Ephesians 4:11-13)
- The foundational gifts (Romans 12:4-8)
- The nine gifts of Holy Spirit (1 Corinthians 12:8-12)

As each has received a spiritual gift (a particular spiritual talent, a gracious divine endowment) employ it for one another as good stewards of God's grace.

1 Peter 4:10 (AMP)

The Five-Fold Gifting / Ascension / Ministry Gifts

In this gifting the people called to these five-fold ministries are the gifts themselves, the representation of Jesus Himself to the body of Christ. They are:

- Apostle
- Prophet
- Evangelist
- Teacher
- Pastor

The Foundational Gifts, Motivational Gifts

We are *all* given gifts *"according to the grace given us"*. Paul likens it to the various organs and limbs in our actual body and how everything works together whilst all are not the same.

These are the seven (Romans 12:4-8):

- Prophecy
- Serving
- Teaching
- Exhortation
- Giving
- Organization
- Mercy

Knowing what our gifting is helps us find our place in the body and helps those in authority over us to place us in the right and functional place. We may operate in a few of these but there will always be one main gifting with which you identify the most closely and in which you have the most success and joy. The one you excel

131

in will touch all your spiritual activity and flow through all of it. For example, if you counsel and your foundational gift is mercy you will be a merciful counsellor. If your gift is teaching and you are a counsellor you will educate as you counsel.

This is how the gifts work together to perfect the church:

- A prophecy-motivated person would ask if the people were being called to repentance sufficiently.
- A server asks if the needs are being met, is often in the kitchen, or outside helping mothers with prams, putting out the chairs, cleaning up when everyone else has gone etc.
- A teacher is passionate about whether the Word is being taught to the people.
- An exhorter will encourage and motivate the people to press on.
- A giver is concerned with needs and finances.
- A mercy person goes to the broken, wounded ones.
- An organizer or administrator will try to organize all of us.

Romans 11:29 talks about the gifts and callings of God being irrevocable and without repentance. He does not change His mind once they are given.

The Gifts of the Holy Spirit

All the gifts of the Holy Spirit operate through love.

If I have prophetic powers and understand all the secret truths and mysteries and possess all knowledge, and sufficient faith to remove mountains, but have not love, I am nothing.

1 Corinthians 13:2 (AMP)

Each Christian receives a spiritual gift when they are filled with the Holy Spirit. God equips us for the ministry He has prepared for us to do. He always pays for what he orders.

There are nine spiritual gifts:

- Word of knowledge
- Word of wisdom
- Discerning of spirits
- Tongues
- Interpretation of tongues
- Prophecy
- Miracles
- Faith
- Healing

THE WORD OF KNOWLEDGE:

The word of knowledge is a word from the knowledge of God that He downloads to us for a particular person, place or situation- in the present and the future. Jesus was using the word of knowledge with the woman at the well (John 4). It is not a gift of knowledge but a small part of the whole. It is not based on the knowledge you already have, for example, from reading the Bible, but it is a gift from God at the time. It can be very powerful in our conversations with people who are not yet Christians as it demonstrates the knowledge that only God can know about a person. If we are ministering at New Age psychic fairs in a prophetic capacity it can stop someone in their tracks as you read their life out to them, highlighting things that only God could know.

It is a very useful evangelistic tool. The word of knowledge can reveal causes of affliction, sickness and demonic oppression. It can reveal God's will for a person's life, demonstrate root problems for situations.

Biblical Examples:

- Saul's lost donkeys are found (1 Samuel 9:20)
- Telling Saul whom he will meet (1 Samuel 10)

133

- God speaks to Ananias and gives him exact directions (Acts 9:11)
- The woman at the well when Jesus reads her life to her with words of knowledge (John 4)

THE WORD OF WISDOM

This is a word from the infinite wisdom of God, usually for a specific time or situation, with which we have no idea what to do unless the Lord shows up and tells us. We are constantly encouraged in the Bible to *"get wisdom"*.

> Get wisdom, get understanding; do not forget my words or swerve from them. Do not forsake wisdom, and she will protect you; love her, and she will watch over you.
>
> *Proverbs 4:5-6 (NIV)*

We are told in Psalm 111 that *"the fear of the Lord is the beginning of wisdom"* (verse 10, NIV) and in Colossians 2:3 that in Christ is hidden *"...all the treasures of wisdom and knowledge"* (NIV).

There are three levels of wisdom: natural worldly wisdom, divine wisdom, and the word of wisdom, the latter being the gift given by God for the body of Christ. No matter what your educational standard has been, God can use you with this gift.

Purposes of the Word of Wisdom:

- To warn of impending danger.
- To affirm a believer in his calling to a ministry.
- To warn of impending disaster, weather patterns, financial crashes.
- To guide in a particular path or action.
- To reveal the thoughts and deep longings of a person's heart.
- To reveal a particular way to pray for someone with a need.
- To reveal lost property, missing persons, solutions to crimes.

Biblical Examples:

- Joseph warns Pharaoh of a famine to come (Genesis 41).
- The burning bush (Exodus 3).
- Solomon and the baby (1 Kings 3:16).
- The specifications for the ark (Genesis 6).
- Lot was warned about Sodom (Genesis 19).
- Moses was instructed to build the tabernacle.

All these gifts are activated through faith. We may see a picture, hear a word, a song, or sense something in which the Holy Spirit urging us on.

DISCERNING OF SPIRITS

Demons often speak through a person. The gift of discernment is required more and more today so we can discern what spirit is operating. It may be demonic or it may be simply our human spirit. You can discern what spirit is attacking you by what you're being accused of. Remember that the devil will always try to get people to do to you what *he* wants to do to you. We can decide to believe many lies about our lives (that we are hopeless cases, will never be able to do what God requires, always be poor and a victim etc.) The demonic realm will always tell us the worst about ourselves and others – but we do need to recognize it and realize that something outside of ourselves is attacking.

God laughs from the heavens at the attempts of the devil to dislodge us, and it is crucial we see positionally that we are in Christ, seated in heavenly places, looking down on the warfare going on. We cannot fail because Jesus always leads us in victory. Our rest in God is a fabulous weapon as we stand still and watch the outcome.

> ...do not put faith in every spirit but test the spirits to discover if they proceed from God.
>
> *1 John 4:1 (NIV)*

Biblical Examples:

- *"...he has a dumb spirit"* – the father discerned correctly (Mark 9:17, AMP).
- *"You are the Christ, the Son of the Living God."* (Matthew 16:16, AMP).
- *"Get behind Me, Satan."* (Matthew 16:23, AMP).
- *"I see {and discern} that you are in the gall of bitterness"* – Peter discerns (Acts 8:23, AMP).
- Paul discerns Elymas's motives – *"You master ... of deception"* – and sends him blind; with the result of the pro-consul receiving salvation (Acts 13:9-12, AMP).
- Paul discerns a spirit of divination and says, *"...come out of her."* (Acts 16:16-18, AMP).

TONGUES:

This is the gift of God through the Holy Spirit for an utterance in an unknown language. The public usage of this gift is in 1 Corinthians 14: 2-4. It is a way to communicate directly with God in praise, worship or intercession. We may also convey a message from God to His people in a public gathering, which hopefully someone will bring an interpretation to.

THE INTERPRETATION OF TONGUES:

This is a Holy Spirit inspired gift given to interpret the meaning and general understanding of an utterance given in tongues, in order to encourage or edify a person or a group.

PROPHECY:

Definition: "The inspired revelation and interpretation of the will and purpose of God concerning a person, place, situation or nation."

It can be spoken, written, sung, danced, acted out, mimed or drawn. God is not limited by His word alone. He is an amazingly diverse God and wants to capture our hearts and our attention in whatever way He can. We are exhorted to *"earnestly desire and cultivate the gifts"* and desire is the key here.

THE WORKING OF MIRACLES:

This is a gift that comes from the heart of God and goes against natural laws, releasing the supernatural into areas like instant healing for diseases, blind eyes seeing, deaf ears opening, limbs growing, miracles of astounding provision such as in the story of the loaves and the fishes, the fish with the gold coin in its mouth, instant weather changes. It is very often accompanied by the gift of faith.

THE GIFT OF FAITH:

This is the gift that is exercised outside of the usual everyday sort of faith and required for particular situations, particularly life and death ones. This gift of faith moves mountains and parts the sea, rolls away rocks, turns a staff into a serpent and water into wine. It enables some to walk on water and believe God for the miraculous.

GIFTS OF HEALING:

This is particularly for the laying on of hands for the relief of pain, disease and trauma. Some Christians seem to have particular anointings from God for different parts of the body, different diseases; things such as back pain, paralysis, chronic fatigue, infertility, legs lengthening etc. We are all, as a body, exhorted to lay hands on the sick and see them recover, and our faith is activated and fuelled as we begin to see successful results. There is no theory or rule, and God remains the Great Physician.

As we continue to press in to all God has with His amazing gifts for us, we are learning to build each other up in love so that Jesus is displayed in all His glory and majesty.

How to Hear Clearly

Like sheep with their shepherd, as we stick close to Him, we hear more clearly. Shutting out the other voices clamouring for our attention in a super-tech world full of media distractions will also be helpful. Learning to be still and wait on the Lord quietly with no hurry is always good. Intimacy will always produce more intimacy. There will always be a battle to spend the much needed time that Jesus deserves to have, and shut out the noise of life for a while. We learn to distinguish the Lord's voice from the devil's voice by becoming more acquainted with the Lord. Knowing His Word is no substitute for knowing Him (or it is like being married and never communicating). If we continually operate from a base of fear, anger and unhealed wounds, we can receive mixed messages. Our healing journey is crucial to our walk with God, and He longs to heal our broken places because He is simply a wonderful and loving Father.

Prayer for Breaking Through in the Gifts of God

"Father, I acknowledge that your precious gifts are for me – your own child – to use both for myself and for others; to build up the body of Christ and to bring a greater level of freedom in the people I minister to wherever they are.

Right now I believe that if I confess my sins, you are faithful and just to forgive me and cleanse me totally, according to 1 John 9.

I cannot earn or deserve these gifts from the Holy Spirit, but they are freely mine by your amazing grace. Because you live in my spirit, Lord Jesus, I have these gifts, and whatever gift I need at the time I will have.

With the authority in the name of Jesus, I command all fear and intimidation to leave me now. I command all unbelief to leave me now, and all remembered pain of past experiences in this area.

I declare I am being equipped for the work of the ministry and I am breaking through all the time in the gifts you have given.

Today, I declare I am a minister of God. I declare I am a prophetic person and I hear from God clearly and accurately. I ask you to sing and speak through me, Lord.

I declare I am a minister of healing, activation and release and that I do not lean on my own understanding but on your arm of faith. I thank you for the blessing you have called me to be as your minister.

Thank you, Lord."

CHAPTER ELEVEN

The Apostle / Prophet Dynamic

Another name for an apostle is "pioneer". A pioneer, according to the Oxford English Dictionary, is "one who goes first into new territories". A pioneer spirit goes forwards and continues on, no matter what. They do not have a settler's mentality but are well able to settle the settlers and then move on to more works of establishing and planting.

There is often a "Gideon factor" with a new work, where the apostle has the vision, and a few are drawn to it, knowing it is God. Generally speaking, most people want to be safe and see that something is going to work, rather than take a risk and hear from God. We have only to look at Mary, a teenage girl entrusted with the birthing of the Messiah, risking public shame and divorce, and Esther, a female, a refugee from an ethnic minority and marginalized, to understand the passion of following the call of God by faith. It is a mistake to believe that the current status quo is necessarily the norm. Jesus is not always into "balanced and normal". God carries within Himself the paradox of being the Lord who does not change but simultaneously instigating change wherever He is.

When God wants to do something amazing he often chooses the weakest of us to show forth His strength. We were not chosen because of our amazing abilities but to display the grace and power of God. Sometimes our talents and natural giftings can get in the way of how God wants to move. In 1 Corinthians 1:26 Paul urges us to *"consider [our] call – not many [of you were considered to be] wise ... influential and powerful..."* (AMP) How true!

Bill Hamon, an apostle/prophet in USA gives this definition:

> "An Apostle is one sent on behalf of another, with the power and authority of the representative coming from the one who sent him ... the continuing ministry of the Apostle is based on how well he conveys the heart and the message of the King."

A "Sending" Spirit

The apostolic spirit is one that is sent by God but also sends out others. Beginning with Moses right through to the present day God has sent his "apostles" (i.e. those sent on behalf of another, God Himself).

Moses was sent to save an entire nation (Exodus 3:14). In fact, all the prophets throughout the entire Bible have been sent to proclaim the oracles and chronicles of God, and still are. Joseph was sent (Psalm 105:26) and his soul entered into the iron of his bondage and the word of the Lord tried and tested him. Elijah was sent (Malachi 4:5) as the prophet of fire, and John the Baptist was sent to proclaim repentance and prepare the way of the Lord.

All the prophets throughout the Old Testament point to Jesus, the greatest "sent one" of all. Jesus then sent out His disciples (Matthew 10:5, Luke 10:1) and then the Holy Spirit was sent out among us (John 14:26). Many of the apostles were "sent ones" (Acts 8:14, 11:22,1 5:22); and the apostles, along with the prophets and the church, sent out others to preach and teach and generally spread the Gospel. (Philippians 2:19, 2:25, 1 Thessalonians 3:2). Most of the epistles in the New Testament begin with words to the effect of "Paul, sent by God..."

The Great Commission

Matthew 28:19-20 and Mark 16:15 describe the great commission of the church to the whole world. It is happening.

141

One of the keys to the success of this great commissioning is in not only knowing you are called but also knowing what you are called to do.

To be commissioned means to go with the authority of another (literally, to be authorized, empowered, appointed and entrusted by that higher authority with the mission given). It is not about evangelism only, but about the preparation of the ground for planting; building and watering the ground, with the long term plan of discipling, teaching and raising up; then sending others out to fulfil their calling. It is very much about raising up works in the Kingdom of God with apostolic Kingdom authority and then moving on, and often being sent by the Lord to do it all again somewhere else. Apostolic anointing is able to achieve prayer that is strategic and authoritative and begins to change world systems and bring the much needed change.

Apostolic ministers have a great sense of their destiny and purpose. They know they have been sent and so, quite simply, they must go. The Holy Spirit manifests all five aspects of the five-fold gifting, with Jesus Himself being the summation of all five.

Apostolic leadership is about character more than anything else. It is about integrity, patience, loyalty and humility. Apostles are consumed with a passion for God's will. They need to have a militant, possessing mentality when breaking through into new ground to establish the Kingdom of God. They know they are sent to take ground from the kingdom of darkness. They know they are to be like Joshua and Caleb, with a strong and different spirit, able to make decisions for many. Apostles are also aware that before the taking of new ground they will encounter giants, demon kings, and fortified cities, often the strongholds in peoples' minds that are religious and rigid.

Often insecure people will look at strength and call it pride but are too insecure to go after it themselves.

We will rule and reign in our lives when we stop depending on others to define us, and go to God, our Father, where our true identity begins. When we stop bending into others, trying to be like them, we will break through into security and maturity. As we stop yielding to the temptation to be manipulating, controlling everyone and everything, we will find our true self as God begins to define us.

Sometimes our strengths and talents can keep us from God rather than our weaknesses. A person with a strong, independent spirit will find it hard to submit, work in a team and depend only on the Lord. As we mature in God, we go from a place of insecurity to allowing God to make us vulnerable, to Him and to others.

Planting and Watering

Planting is about pioneering, breaking new ground and establishing life. Apostles plant churches and establish new works in God. Then, like any General back from battle, they go home, rest, and report back to the base, then move on to other sheep in other pastures. They then tend to revisit and "water" those works already established. Jesus, the Lord of the harvest, will always bless what He has planted, but is under no obligation to bless what He has not. Because the apostolic call is about training and releasing, secure apostolic men and women will take great joy in raising up teams of people and taking them to a new work that has been planted.

Many churches will also birth illegitimate apostolic offspring, which will call themselves "apostolic" whilst not embracing prophets or the prophetic, and functioning very much on their own agenda. If we do not have the true, we will never recognize the false.

Apostolic sending involves much travel and a requirement to stay as long or as short a time as God requires.

In 2000, the Lord sent me to England, where I was involved for seven years in teaching, training and establishing people both in the prophetic and in restoration healing. The work was greatly contested, and there were many battles. Some we won and some we took a few hits in – but we learnt a lot about warfare and holding ground. A prophetic company of people was formed, and I was involved in teaching prophetic schools and restoration healing schools, and training others up to carry it on after I had left. People began to be greatly blessed by the Lord as they began to deal with their wounds, traumas and issues, and become healthy emotionally, spiritually and physically. People began to move geographically and reposition themselves where God was "happening", albeit in a small way.

When we are weak, sick and poor, we are no threat to the enemy and we are easy to control. When we are well, strong and have finances, we can do a lot in establishing things in God's Kingdom.

Paul's Sending

After Paul's incredible "road to Damascus" encounter, he began to travel. He went to Antioch for a year; then to Corinth for eighteen months, and then on to Ephesus for two years at the School of Tyrannus (Acts 19:9) where he held discussions in the lecture room from 10am until 3pm. Apostolic work is demanding and taxing, but God promises that *"he who waters shall himself be watered"* (Proverbs 11:25, AMP).

The goal of planting and watering is tangible: obvious increase, to present a field to God. It is about working quietly and diligently through storms and darkness, simply being faithful to what God has called a person to do.

Apostles invest their lives, their time and their money into the Kingdom of God.

Communication is Vital

Effective communication is vital to the work. Apostles build relationships and friendships with other five-fold ministers, and this is the networking that God would have them do. Five-fold ministers who are sold out to establishing the Kingdom of God will always be greatly used in mending nets, where there has been an offence or a wounding or misunderstanding, and are dedicated to letting the "kingdom of ego" die , going out of their way to keep the nets whole and mended.

Apostles continually bring forth present truth, reproof, correction in love, and instruction in the Word. They preach, teach and minister in the spirit and will spend hours preaching, teaching and prophesying.

They use three primary vehicles to communicate truth effectively:

- Vocal ministry: *"...that I may open my mouth ... boldly..."* (Ephesians 6:19, AMP)
- Written ministry through manuals, books, teaching resources
- Auditory, through DVDs and CDs

Summary of What an Apostle Does

- They set up strong teams to oversee the church while they themselves are away planting and watering.
- They ordain and commission others into their calling.
- They are able to "set" people into their ministries and calling and impart the anointing to do so.
- They coordinate other ministries to flow together for the sake of unity.
- They are constantly administrating and delegating, setting people and groups together, matching people with places and needs.
- They are problem solvers where there are leadership issues, violation of conduct, doctrinal issues or financial issues.
- An apostle plants and waters first and foremost and has the Father's heart.
- They oversee, establish, parent, reprove, ordain and network.

The Signs of an Apostle

PATIENCE:

> Indeed, the signs that indicate a [genuine] apostle were performed among you fully and most patiently in miracles and wonders and mighty works.
>
> *2 Corinthians 12:12 (AMP)*

Patience is about character being formed by all the events which are allowed by God. Character will *always* be more important to the Lord than gifting. Patience is about remaining steadfast and immovable in adversity.

Patience is in staying anchored when all around you is in chaos. It is in manning a post and fulfilling a duty, simply "being there", in spite of everything. The writer of Hebrews encourages us to *"run with perseverance the race marked out for us"* (Hebrews 12:1, AMP).

In Acts 20:24, Paul demonstrated the patience that has been wrought in him through years of difficulties and hardship when he wrote, *"...none of these things move me; neither do I esteem my life dear to myself, if only I may finish my course with joy..."* (AMP)

ENDURANCE:

Because of the pressure of this office, learning to endure hardship with patience is vital.

In 1 Corinthians 4:9, Paul talks about the life lived by the early apostles. They worked day and night, faced hostile authorities, defended their apostleship, and battled demonic hordes. Nothing much has changed in many ways. Simply by being an active apostle there will be spiritual attacks, discomfort of all kinds and religious persecution. They saw themselves as love slaves of Jesus, enduring a life of testing by many persecutions.

Those who answer the apostolic call must learn to patiently endure suffering and be able to withstand pressure. A leader cannot lead unless people follow. Nor can he demand a response just because of his own calling.

The apostolic anointing speaks of a pioneering spirit with a breakthrough dynamic. Pioneers are men and women with courage, tenacity and vision. They initiate happenings and breakthrough into new areas and new truths regardless of cost and unpopularity.

Ongoing, sustained apostolic preaching brings breakthroughs in finances, media, economics, politics, corporate affairs, land development projects, to name a few.

Apostolic ministry is trail-blazing and opens up territory for others to follow. It is a rallying anointing, a gathering anointing, to draw together the army of the Lord across geographical regions and nations. It is a ministry of warfare. It resists all the powers of darkness and penetrates new areas with the light of the Lord Jesus Christ.

NETWORKS AND NETWORKING

Definition: "A band of autonomous churches and individual churches that are voluntarily united into an organized structure."

A network will have a common vision and express active apostolic ministry. The strength undergirding it will be the relationships, through the Father's love; how we relate to one another will always be more important than what we do.

The main problem that I see in the new networks that are now forming is that of denominationalism. If we are coming into a new dimension of church government because of the emergence of apostles and the whole apostolic movement, what does this mean for the current structures of the church, such as denominations?

There is no actual biblical basis for a denomination but only for a local church in whatever form that takes, whether it be in a house, on the beach, or in a building. The structures upholding most denominations prevent true networking from happening. Denominations and hierarchal structures that are controlling are neither biblical nor effective. They undermine the true unity that the body needs to function. This can only lead to division and a breakdown in communication.

I believe the answer is that God does not violate the biblical principles of authority nor bring a violation of them but rather a fulfilment of them for greater unity between the diverse camps in the body.

Apostles are able to work within local churches, and their leaders never override the local authority. The "generals" (apostles) are accountable mutually to each other. That can mean submission upwards and across. This, then, becomes a relational network where leaders maintain openness, communication and teachability. When leaders come to the end of themselves, God can begin.

The Kingdom of God is a huge net, and with the advent of the World Wide Web, millions of people can now be reached, informed taught and ministered to.

A network is simply an extension of the team ministry bringing together five-fold ministers and leaders, along with the people, in a way to establish the Kingdom of God. True apostles are happy and willing to merge their gifts with others' and not necessarily have a name or claim to anything but let God have all the glory.

Servant Leaders

An apostolic team is one of servant-leaders who facilitate the team's vision and activate its purpose. Their networks are founded and continued in relationships of love. Anything built on rigid rules and control is destined to fail. Free time spent together perpetuates this networking. It is the difference between an organization and an organism. Importantly, too, the apostle maintains fellowship outside his main stream.

When any member becomes relationally dislocated, the net becomes torn because the net is made of relationships. Only clean nets catch fish so the net needs to have frequent removal of barnacles, slime and other debris. When the "net" gets too tattered we need to hone our gifts, update and improve for greater effectiveness. When we dislocate, then isolate away from the body for long periods of time, we can become polluted with delusional thinking and missed communications.

An essential component to unity is to fellowship together as often as possible, building up the unity in the binding power of peace.

The net needs to be cast where the fish will be caught. Every net has to be immersed in communities so we can cast ourselves with total abandonment into a sea of lost humanity.

It is only as we allow the old, religious, dodo-dead dinosaur model of the church, that never equips, to die off that we can move into the present day of the Lord with excitement and anticipation at His soon coming.

The Importance of Reproduction

We must continually reproduce ourselves and duplicate ourselves and our ministry in others of like mind and spirit. If no mentoring or training occurs it will die. The race that we run with perseverance is a relay race, where we have to hand on the baton (the things that we know, that we are gifted with) to the ones we have been raising up, so the race can be continued and everyone wins.

Types of Apostles

Some people believe that when the twelve apostles (those who were with Jesus) died, so did apostolic ministry. However, like the other four of the five-fold, it is a perpetual ministry, and has no more died than has the pastoral, prophetic, evangelistic or teaching. God continues to this day and will continue to establish five-fold ministry in the church.

Apostles were the first to be activated and the last to be restored.

Some of the types of apostles are:

- Apostles of certain truths: Martin Luther, Smith Wigglesworth
- Apostles of faith: Kenneth Hagin, Kenneth Copeland
- Apostles of the truth of healing: Oral Roberts, Benny Hinn, Kathryn Kuhlmann, John G. Lake
- Apostles of the truth about the prophetic: Bill Hamon, Cindy Jacobs
- Apostles of evangelism: Oral Roberts, Billy Graham
- Apostles of regions, nations: Reinhardt Bonnke, Gladys Aylward
- The apostles that God is raising up today are like Paul, who walked in humility but acted in boldness.

Paul's Progression:

"I am as good as any of the apostles."
↓
Five years later: *"I am the least of the apostles."*
↓
Later still: *"I am the least of the saints...."*
↓
Five years on: *"I am the greatest of sinners..."*

True humility allows the apostle to carry His anointing, embrace it, act on it and in it. God will always resist the proud and give grace to the humble. The higher the calling, the deeper the foundations need to be dug. We are constantly learning, gleaning, discerning, becoming, and being changed from glory to glory. I constantly ask God for *"a spirit of wisdom and revelation ... in the ... knowledge of Him"* (Ephesians 1:17, AMP).

He must continually increase and I must decrease. My Kingdom, the Kingdom of my ego, *has* to go to establish more and more of the Kingdom of God in every facet of life. Our first government will always be self-government, where we learn to approach all of life from the spirit-man perspective rather than the soul perspective only.

Apostolic Building

When a church or a ministry is built by apostolic anointing, rather than pastoral, it will be built with strength and effectiveness. After a good foundation has been built, then structure can form. Many valid works of God are hidden away from the eyes of men until the foundations are established strongly. The foundations will always be about building strong relationships, birthed and nurtured in the agape love of God. After being "dungeoned" for what might seem forever, God then allows a work to be seen and heard. It's all in the timing of God.

The government of God is on the shoulders of the apostle; there can be an oversight of ministries, churches, regions, nations. Paul was well able to bring down demonic strongholds. It is a "Samson" anointing; a crushing, ripping, gate-removing anointing. "Gates" speak of entry points. The spirit of Samson is the word "Saliac" which means "to come in force, violently".

Apostles are fathers and mothers to the other five-fold ministers, and in this mode they reproduce after their own kind.

Prophets and apostles must be released to be itinerant, not residential. Evangelists are the same, and in fact their mission field will always be the unchurched pre-Christians who are not going to be found in churches.

Pastors are "habitation-minded", as are teachers. The other three of the five-fold are "visitation-minded"

Apostolic Establishing

In Romans 1:11 Paul says, *"I am yearning to see you, that I may impart ... some spiritual gift to strengthen and establish you."* (AMP)

An establishing anointing comes through an apostle when he or she becomes part of a church, a ministry. Truth is established, direction comes, order comes, gifts are imparted and the work moves forward.

Apostles are essential to the church in this time we are in to simply get everything moving in the right direction. Whereas prophets prophesy a thing, a situation, a truth into the atmosphere, the apostle will establish it and put backbone into it. Apostolic faith is fierce, bold and daring. It does not deliberate and procrastinate and wait till everyone feels good about it. They know the times and the seasons of God and say, "Let's go! Let's do it!" Whatever God calls us to, He will equip us in. He always pays for what He orders.

Power Gifts

Apostles are the ones who classically raise the dead and do miracles of healing following strong and accurate words of knowledge. These power gifts are, of course, not confined to apostles. The other five-fold ministers are able to use these gifts, particularly the prophet and the evangelist, but they seem to be the God-given attributes that belong to apostolic authority.

Apostles tend to move into an area and stay while establishing God's government in that area or region. Where prophets sniff out, discern, hear, see, sense and point out, ideally they can then hand on all that information to the apostle who can then act on it. Prophets see, apostles do.

Apostles will bring strong job identity. They know who does what and when.

Prophets love their solitude and simply *must* have time alone with the Lord. They sometimes force themselves to be social and not be so aloof, but generally prefer to "do the job" and retreat back to obscurity. Prophetically centred churches tend to focus on worship, warfare, correction and direction in the spirit. This is not a "one size fits all" type of church, and people leave because they don't want lengthy prophetic worship or the exposure in them sometimes of what God wants to heal. It's all about preference, rather than rightness or wrongness. Many do not want to change their personal status quo or learn how to fight the giants that stand in the way of the possession of their land of promise from God.

Many are called but not everyone makes the choice to follow the call of God on their life and to be truly owned by Him. The price is high; it is your will and your life. Not all come to the knowledge that we are truly "not our own" but His. This is the knowledge that you walk with when you choose to say *yes* to the calling of God. The time between the calling and the release is crucial. Called people know they are called, and they are simply different because of that. They view everything from the perspective of the will of God and the establishing of His Kingdom.

Apostolic Churches

An apostolic church is one that understands God's order and government. It is a church with a pioneering spirit and a breakthrough dynamic. Pioneers are men and women with courage, tenacity and vision. Like the pioneers who travelled hundreds of miles to break open a nation, putting their lives on the line, called people surrender everything to follow the King.

Apostolic ministers initiate happenings and make a way into new areas and new truths regardless of cost and often unpopularity. God has the perfect plan to ensure that it will always be about His name, His fame, His Glory.

Apostolic preaching opens up areas for others to move into. It is always about serving the One who has sent you. Whereas prophets speak and demonstrate the message of the King, the apostle brings it into establishment.

> God has appointed first apostles...
>
> *1 Corinthians 12:28 (NIV)*

The Greek word "proton" means "first in time, in place, in order, in importance". Apostles are prototypes and initiate things never seen before.

The apostolic ministry is one of warfare, resisting the powers and principalities of darkness, and penetrating new areas with light. It is like the difference between the "Moses anointing" of prophet/pastor and the "Joshua anointing" that saw then conquered giants, demon kings and fortified cities in the Promised Land.

What's the Issue Here?

Apostles are issue-orientated, not need-orientated as a pastor-shepherd is. They are consumed with bringing corrective change without compromise, so that the church will line up with the Word of God.

Apostolic ministry is concerned with the condition of the church. It thrives in persecution, is often called rebellious and trouble-making, but apostles are compelled to bring reform despite opposition. They will defend and confirm truth. They will stand when truth is attacked and all have deserted.

The Seal of the Apostle

> Even though I may not be an apostle to others, surely I am to you! For you are the seal of my apostleship in the Lord.
>
> *1 Corinthians 9:2 (NIV)*

The visible living seal or symbol of true apostleship ministry is that of the people birthed and raised by that ministry. This is the apostolic company of believers who will demonstrate apostolic characteristics. They will be stamped and sealed in it. In past times, the seal, usually by a signet ring into wax, declared its trueness, its authenticity. So, too, with the apostolic seal.

Summary of Functions

To sum up, the functions of an apostle are:

- To gather for the purposes of teaching, training and mobilizing people to fulfil the purposes of God.
- To impart whichever spiritual gift is required.
- To mobilize the Army of God, to then be sent out to fulfil the great commission.

- To bring order into churches and ministries, corporations and companies with God-given governmental authority.
- To bring correction in areas of false teaching and rebellious behaviour.
- To bring in reform, usher in reformation into the postmodern church, without religious denominationalism.
- To spend long periods of time building into people, especially in foundational areas.
- To teach truth with revelation.
- To preach dynamically, accompanied with signs, wonders, miracles.
- To parent, always with the Father's heart, which establishes identity (Malachi 4, 1 Corinthians 4:15).
- To initiate new works, new ideas, moving on from old ways of doing things and encouraging others to embrace present truth for the present day, being totally relatable to the culture.
- To wage warfare in unseen realms; pulling down demonic strongholds and establishing God's Kingdom. The word "warfare" is from the Greek "strateia" meaning "apostolic career".
- To ordain into certain ministries and works, by the laying on of hands and impartation, either alone or with a company of other apostles and prophets.
- To confront pride, selfish ambition, witchcraft, immorality, false teaching and any other enemy to the precious body of Christ.

Comings and Goings

When God gives the apostle a "reach" – that is, a territory, a people group, a church or a geographical area – and there are still major flaws in character or many wounds not dealt with, there will be major repercussions for the apostle and all those around him or her. If they have not addressed their prejudices, religious preferences or old mind-sets, they may compromise the culture they have been sent to. For example, the Lord may send an apostle to a community that embraces the New Age, hippie lifestyle, a drug and alcohol related community or an ethnic third world region.

Open doors left open will attract an enemy attack. Open wounds attract flies (i.e. the demonic realm).

Authority attracts persecution. We can be unpopular simply because of the call on our life.

A spiritual atmosphere over a city is made up of the ruling demonic principality (i.e. what dominates the people of the city), the spiritual history of the region, and the Holy Spirit of God in the church presence of that area. When an apostolic work is being established, there may be territorial antagonism from the religious establishment, even mockery and hostility. Often people mock what they do not understand. Everyone needs to get in on the work. When we read the book of Nehemiah, we see that as they all co-laboured together, *"everyone worked with one hand and held a weapon with the other hand"* (Nehemiah 4:17, AMP).

We need to keep the vision before us and not go into logic and reason. Both will destroy faith. Wondering is wavering.

It's all about sticking to the plan, the task, the issue, and this is going on to maturity.

Apostles need to establish the church from the foundations up and build it strong, then go on to do the next thing. Unlike the pastor, who stays and stays to shepherd the people well, the apostle is *not* called in the same way at all. They must raise up strong apostolic teams – some to be sent, and some to maintain the church when others are away. They certainly love with the heart of the Father but are called to "go ye" rather than "stay ye".

So we can see that the ministry of the apostle did not die when the twelve died, but as with all five-fold it is still to *some*. Just because we understand a particular gift/office does not necessarily mean we have it, but if it *is* you then accept it, embrace it and *be it!*

If it's not you, support those who are called to this office, in the same way; if you're not called to the nations, then support those who are.

We support them in prayer and in finances. Often the nation you intercede for is one you might go to because you already go there in the spirit.

Don't get distracted just because some prefer the pastoral anointing compared to the prophetic. Be who you are, move when God says. This is merely what is called "doctrines of preference".

In these times the calling and mantle of many is changing, and it can be a lonely and confusing time. We will never be successful in our obedience to God if we are still trying to please everyone else.

> Now am I trying to win the favour of men, or of God? If I were still seeking popularity with men I should not be a bond servant of God.
>
> *Galatians 1:10 (NIV)*

The Enemies of an Apostle

Pressure causes the apostle to come alive. There are enemies, who come to every individual office, as I have explained in an earlier chapter. Just as the enemies to the prophet are Jezebel, fear, rejection, and a persecution complex, the apostolic office draws its own enemies too.

WITCHCRAFT:

Apostolic authority will always confront and overthrow this spirit. There will always be much rebellion and disobedience to the Word and to godly, delegated authority in a church where this spirit is allowed to operate. "Bewitching" is slow, insidious and subtle, never obvious. Like a slow-acting anaesthetic it will gradually cause churches that started in the spirit to end in the flesh or to go from great liberty into legalism, like the Galatian church (Galatians 3:1-3).

The aim of witchcraft in the church is to water down the power of the Word of God and ultimately destroy biblical Christianity.

157

Apostles and prophets will always be on the battlefront against this spirit. Apostles may act on what the prophets see, sense, feel and hear in the spirit.

What is witchcraft? It is counterfeit authority which often uses control, coercion and manipulation to dominate. It starts in the flesh (Galatians 5:20) and is quickly empowered demonically. Basic witchcraft is exhibited when we use any power other than the Holy Spirit to bring about an outcome. It comes in many forms, such as emotional pressure and hype in a church or a person. Everything we do that is rooted in hype, emotional manipulation or control, even if it appears to be good and noble, is doomed to fail because it is motivated by counterfeit spiritual authority (i.e. witchcraft).

Even when the flesh looks good, it will always war against the spirit. Hype is simply excitement without quite knowing why. Zeal is altogether different and can be a God-given attribute.

SELFISH AMBITION:

Definition: "An ungodly drive to be the best and the first, zeal without love, a striving to be first and best and top dog." Selfish ambition brings the "yoke of man" on the people.

Ambition can drive the people mercilessly (Ezekiel 34) into good works and community projects, until they are exhausted and suffer from burnout.

Most churches have a proportion of people who do not know how to say no, but are caught up in a co-dependent "need to be needed" type of pleasing. It is a thin line between that and true servanthood.

Selfish ambition, when it is birthed in a leader, can lie, cheat, steal and connive, just to be successful. Ambition follows a Saul-type leader not a David, and easily loses sight of grace and mercy.

The most classic example of selfish ambition is found in Genesis 11:4 when the people said, *"Come let us build us a city and a tower whose top reaches into the sky, and let us make a name for ourselves..."* (AMP)

Other Bible verses on this theme are 3 John 9-10, Daniel 3:1-7, and Matthew 23:12.

Ambition, pride and competitiveness can be in all of us, and until we surrender totally to the dealings of God in our lives we cannot be effective in God.

I believe the Lord will always be far more interested in the forming of our character to be conformed to His, than the development of our gifting.

Jesus taught in Mark 12:28 about the dangers of being like the Scribes who were constantly looking for the accolades of man, recognition and the front row in the church. Paul admonishes us in Philippians 1:27 that our conduct and manner of living will be counted worthy of Christ, and that we will stand firm, united in spirit.

Ambition can be ruthless and can kill its own! Fathers don't kill but promote their children to do better, to have more, to go further. Selfish ambition has a hireling mentality not a Father's heart.

Control follows ambition, rooted in insecurity and often rejection.

COMPETITION:

Definition: "To rival, contend with, be opposed to, contest, run against."

The opposite is to promote others, defer to others, to stay hidden away if God is telling you to. It's not about how many, how big, how much but how you honour others around you. Your strength is exhibited in how you bear with the weak ones (Romans 15:1).

ISOLATION:

Isolation often follows after wounding. Pressure causes the insecure to leave a work or a project early before it is completed. Isolation can be a breeding ground for paranoia, rejection and suspicion.

When we "dis-member" ourselves from the body of Christ, we can be open to delusion. Even though we can be wounded in relationship, we can also be healed through relationship. A lot of what we think is discernment can simply be suspicion. If people don't agree with your vision that God gave, don't isolate from them. Instead, love them,, and keep your arms open to them, pray and bless them.

Apostolic ministry is lonely and isolating, so it is important for apostles to stay linked in to the body, as amputated limbs can only die. It is important not to let isolation into your heart. The desire to fellowship breaks the power of isolation. We all need to get our wounds healed so we can get back on board.

PRIDE:

Pride is the worst sin of all, and is what made Satan "Satan". God always resists pride (1 Peter 5:5).

JEALOUSY:

Jealousy is actually a "trust of God" issue – that "someone might have more". Jealousy is the desire to protect what we think we have for fear that someone may take it away from us.

Envy is a deep, resentful desire to have what someone else has. It is rooted in fear and lack of trust in God.

THE FEAR OF MAN:

It is vital to fear God more than the people or the circumstances or we will fall from true spiritual authority. In 1 Samuel 13:11, Saul said, *"I saw that the people were scattering from me..."* (AMP)

We must stand until the next order comes from the King. It is one battle to take the ground but another to maintain it. We usually lose the war in the second place not the first, therefore maintaining is everything.

Proverbs 29:25 says, *"The fear of man brings a snare."* (AMP) The trap *is* the fear. It will cause us to pre-empt the plan of God, to manipulate and control as we start pleasing people instead of God. Eventually we cannot hear the voice of the Holy Spirit and instead obey the voice of man.

Prophets and apostles are particularly called to teach the people to hear from God themselves. We are not to strive after positions of authority but accept the responsibilities that are God-given.

Going Beyond Your Anointing or Sphere of Responsibility

Often Satan will push us out beyond our ability to cause us to fall, fail and be ridiculed. When we are operating in some of these "entry points" it is tempting to go beyond what God is saying to do.

God may call us to mentor/disciple three or four people, and we may take on twelve people that were not given to us by God. We can burn out, blame God, blame the people, but ultimately God says, "My yoke is easy, My burden light." We may go beyond a designated geographical region and we go beyond the grace of God. It takes a knowing of the grace of God and humility to walk in true spiritual authority. We must decrease; He must increase.

As the true apostles of God are released to take their place in the body of Christ globally, they will be like the spine, bringing support and the much-needed alignment to the whole body. Just as the prophets are representative of the senses of the body, so the apostles are the Father's heart and the spine which, when in proper alignment, will cause the whole church to rise up, to move, and to go forward.

CHAPTER TWELVE

The Jezebel Power

It is no surprise to know that every one of the five-fold gifts has a specific enemy that comes to damage, disempower and generally cause havoc in lives. The enemy to the prophet and all those who are prophetic is the Jezebel power.

To the apostle the archenemy seems to be Babylon and all things pertaining to world systems, political systems and whatever is committed against the establishment of Kingdom rule and the authority of Jesus Christ.

Five-fold teachers will battle against religious mind-sets and confusion, and the evangelist will fight carnality and the comforts that come from everywhere but the Holy Spirit. The pastor will often battle against rejection and his own victim spirit.

When a church or a person begins to pick up their prophetic calling, almost immediately the devil seems to send in a Jezebel spirit to harass and destroy, control and intimidate. It will operate most effectively in the presence of an "Ahab", that is, a passive male or female. (The story of Ahab and Jezebel is in 1 Kings 16:29-33.)

Origins and Short History

Every city, state, nation or geographical area has its own organization in the spirit realm of principalities and powers. The spirit realm in a place consists of the history in the land, the Kingdom of God presently being established in the area and the kingdom of darkness being established.

A principality seems to be limited by geography. A power, however, appears to have dominion over pervading evil influences and realms and is not bound by geography. Jezebel is a power that operates globally. As with all spiritual forces it needs a host to operate through – human beings.

Where Does Jezebel Come From?

She was the daughter of Ethbaal (1 Kings 16:31) who ruled the Sidonians for thirty-two years as a priest-king. Baal was an ancient male divinity involving sun worship, the first rays of the rising sun and the last as it was going down. Ethbaal was also a high priest of Ashtoreth, a female divinity representing Venus and also a Moon goddess involving extreme sexual impurity.

Jezebel married Ahab, a weak, indulgent puppet-king, controlled by her to the point of his committing murder for gain. In 1 Kings 16:33 it says that Ahab did more to provoke the Lord to anger than all the kings before him. They brought Israel into the captivity of the idolatry of Baal and Ashtoreth worship both representative of extreme sexual immorality and the control of the nation through this.

Jezebel killed hundreds of God's prophets until Elijah confronted her and slaughtered her prophets at Mount Carmel. She was eventually thrown from an upstairs window by her own male eunuchs, who popped their heads out of the window when Jehu, the newly anointed King of Israel, shouted up to them, "Who is on my side?" The story is told in 2 Kings 9 of her grisly end, where only her skull, her feet and the palms of her hands remained.

The Main Aims of Jezebel Power

Her main purpose is to shut down the prophetic voice of Jesus in the church. It is also to control churches, marriages, ministries and people through fear and intimidation.

This spirit seduces sexually, and is often alluring and full of charm, which God calls "deceitful" in Proverbs 31. It is an anti-anointing, anti-Christ spirit operating.

Main Targets

It targets sensitive, prophetic people who are full of fear and want to please. It will target men with a weakness for pornography. It targets pastors, prophetic musicians, and anointed artists. It is perfectly matched by a man or woman with an Ahab spirit and can convince the other person to compromise to wrongdoing.

We are most open to an attack of Jezebel after a great victory. Remember when Elijah had his greatest all-time victory and slew all the priests of Baal? He ran for his life from Jezebel and was so depressed and intimidated he wanted to take his own life. This power is emasculating to men and disempowers in subversive, subtle ways so it can control and dominate.

The last reference to Jezebel is in Revelation 17:1 and 19:2 where she is described as being *"seated on many waters"* (AMP) i.e. peoples, multitudes and nations. In verses 5 and 6 of chapter 17 she is described as being *"the mother of prostitutes and of the abominations of the earth ... drunk with the blood of God's holy people, the blood of those who bore testimony to Jesus"* (NIV).

God will allow her persecution until he burns her by fire. In Revelation 18:8 we read that *"she will be consumed by fire, for mighty is the Lord God who judges her"* (NIV). There is an end to her reign.

The Characteristics of Jezebel in the Church

When the Jezebel spirit is operating within a church, a spirit of false prophecy can prevail which is deceptive and controlling.

There will be discouragement with the people, religiosity, fear and very little Holy Spirit anointing released. It will stop the true worship of Jesus and the release of the prophetic gifting. It will always stir up division, confused communications between people and put one person against another by secret suggestions and gossip.

It is like a double-sided coin. The derivation of the name "Jezebel" comes from two words: "friend, companion" on the one side and "murderer" on the other side. Like the Ashtoreth symbol it is two-faced: the lily on one side and the serpent on the other.

This spirit hates authority over it, must control, never bows and must undermine all God-given authority. It must be large and in charge. It pretends submission to get its own way.

It often looks great, sounds great, has a nice façade or image, and is often very talented and gifted musically or administratively. It will support the leadership with lip-service, but not with the right motives of the heart. It needs position, title, a name on the door, accolades that go beyond godly honouring. It loves to be seen, recognized and noticed. It loves weak men and women who are easy to control. It loves what we call "yes men" who never disagree with it. It always has intimidated passive and unwhole people surrounding it. It uses intimidation and threats, manipulation and seduction to get its own way and control everything.

This spirit always brings striving, with lots of contention swirling around it. A person carrying a Jezebel spirit will come with their own agenda, which is not necessarily the agenda of the church leadership. They will be seemingly in agreement but only on the surface, to climb up the ladder to the top. They will be dissenting and divisive and critical of leadership behind closed doors, often prefacing their sentences with, "I don't want to be critical, but..." and launch into their own perspective of things that are considered "wrong".

There is usually a strong streak of jealousy and envy – hidden but always there, couched behind a big smile.

In a church, too, this spirit in a person can fantasize about the pastor and imagine herself being the pastor's wife (obviously if the pastor is male) and can even put a death wish on the pastor's wife which, if undetected, can lead to sickness and prolonged ill health. The spouse is often unaware of all this and particularly if a woman carrying Jezebel is openly flirting with half the men in the church. The women, who are emotionally more tuned in than men anyway, will say to their man, "She's flirting with you!" to which they generally reply, "Nonsense! I never noticed a thing."

Sometimes a woman carrying Jezebel power will intimidate the pastor's wife to remove her from a particular scene. She will use flattery and seduction, charm and charisma, and manoeuvre herself to get as close to the leadership as possible. This then can become witchcraft in the church, based on control and manipulation and nothing to do with the Holy Spirit. They often want to control the finances in the church, and therefore almost "run" the church.

You can never quite nail what it is they are doing underhandedly but you know it is there, very insidious and subversive. This spirit brings depression, discouragement and causes you to want to leave the ministry, just as the effect was on Elijah the prophet. Psalm 55:21,22 sums it up: *"...smooth words but war in the heart."*

Jezebel in a Marriage

In a marriage it is "my way or the highway" and it will not back down. The Jezebel spirit is demanding and domineering and is, in fact, a bully. Underlying all this is a deep fear of rejection, stemming from an earlier rejection history, where a decision or a vow is made to own control and intimidate before it is done to them.

There is, too, a fear of emotional abandonment; coupled with an inability to forgive and often a total lack of having experienced unconditional love and the grace of God. Sexual perversion is often found in a marriage where Jezebel dominates.

Jezebel in a Man

Jezebel men tend to palm off to their wives the over-responsibility of being priest and prophet, whilst being insensitive to the emotional needs of their wives and never nurturing. They are usually harsh cruel and controlling.

In a man this is called misogyny, literally "the hatred of women". The hatred and dishonouring of women is a double sided coin; on the one side the desire to please through fear and then shame at the fear, and on the other side the need to control the wife whom they perceive to have power and who must at any cost be disempowered. Misogyny operates because of areas of wounding that have not been dealt with, either from an overbearing mother or female authority figure or following the example of a misogynist father.

The wounds are also often rooted in the deep fear of abandonment by a woman, so restricting steps are put in place to ensure it never happens. Sometimes misogynist men will remove their wife and family geographically to ensure they are dependent on the husband totally and extended family is nowhere near. Jezebel husbands function ideally when their wife is wounded and passive and never says no.

Jezebel in a Woman

In a woman there can be a despising, even mockery, of men and a refusal to submit to any authority, either male or female. Again this spirit is most effective when married to an Ahab personality.

I am sure you have met this in people in all sorts of places whether it is in a church, a job or a marriage. It must not be mixed up with a strong, confident person that comes simply from being secure in one's own identity. It is certainly *not* a woman who wears lots of make-up on her face!

When Jezebel operates through a woman there will be a strong control spirit with an underlying intimidation, sometimes accompanied by threats. She will not submit at any cost even to a godly man; this effectively undermines his God-ordained authority. These women make all the decisions without consultation with their husband, particularly financial; always answer for their husband and finish his sentences for him; correct him publicly and say things like, "Well, this is what the real story is..." to generally keep him passive and looking a fool in front of people. When a woman or a man takes on a role not given by God, it paves the way for spiritual deception. The children in this family will be confused and bewildered, and often walk away from the Lord.

A woman through whom a Jezebel spirit operates will often withhold sexual contact in a marriage as a punishment, and sex can be used as a reward for "good behaviour".

I believe this is one of the meanings of 'defrauding' in 1 Thessalonians 4:3-6 and 1 Corinthians 7:5; that is, withholding something from a person that is not yours to withhold.

Results of Jezebel Influence

In every place that we have been dominated and controlled we can sustain fragmentation of our soul: our mind, our will, our emotions.

Where men have been under a strong Jezebel power from a parent, a wife or a leader, they can be "double minded" and so "unstable in all their ways" (James 1:8). Jezebel's effects are weakness, passivity and indecision.

This power will operate through angry, bitter women who have been abused by the misuse of authority over them. There can be a strong jealousy and malice towards you and the prophetic call on your life, the anointing you carry or the ministry God has given you. It will always bring division in a church, a marriage, a community or a friendship.

Jezebel hates the prophet and the prophet hates this power. We do not, however, fight against flesh and blood, and we have only one enemy, which is *not* each other. Jezebel will particularly attack true prophetic ministry, to shut down the voice of God.

How It Comes In

It comes in through rejection wounding. Satan wounds us, and our silent vows keep the wound open. The vow taken, almost subconsciously, is, "No-one will ever do this to me again." Most people who operate in this spirit are deeply rejected people with unattended wounds. They can be "a lamb at church and a roaring lion at home" sort of personality, with double standards and two faces.

What Jezebel Hates

This spirit hates prophets and prophetic ministers, particularly when religious facades and rituals are exposed as the emptiness they are. She hates free-flowing, radical, extravagant worship of Jesus, intercession that shuts her down, and male authority that is God-ordained and full of humility and servanthood. She hates boldness in the Holy Spirit, as this can be the spirit of Jehu running her to the ground.

So what do we do about it?

Let's start with a couple of scriptures.

> In [this] freedom Christ has made us free [and completely liberated us]; stand fast then, and do not be hampered and held ensnared and submit again to a yoke of slavery [which you have once put off].
>
> *Galatians 5:1 (AMP)*

> Do you not know that if you continually surrender yourselves to anyone to do his will, you are slaves of him whom you obey...
>
> *Romans 6:16 (AMP)*

Remember, Jezebel is a spirit power, not a woman. Remember, too, that the Holy Spirit is greater and more powerful than any anti-Christ power. *"You, dear children, are from God and have overcome them, because the one who is in you is greater than the one who is in the world."* (1 John 4:4, NIV).

It is always right and tremendously helpful to pray, and if you do not confront this spirit, you give it a license to take more and more ground in your life, stifling your prophetic gifting. If you do not confront it, it continues to bring division, disruption and much discouragement. When we have been under the effect of a Jezebellic person we can feel utterly discouraged, depressed and want to leave our ministry.

Jezebel works against the prophet but also can work through unwhole, rejected prophetic people with unattended emotional wounds. But the good news is:

> God disarmed the principalities and powers that were raged against us and made a bold display of them, triumphing over them in the cross.
>
> *Colossians 2:15 (AMP)*

Jesus has triumphed over all powers and broken all curses. He has taken every sin and sickness on the Cross. It is as we apply this truth by faith that we ourselves are freed. Many times, generational iniquities can affect our lives from one generation to the next and the Jezebel spirit can be passed down the generations to us. As we acknowledge the sins of the generations before us, that are affecting our lives now, and forgive parents and grandparents that have sinned in the past, renouncing off any bondage, we are free. And free indeed.

Prayer to Renounce Jezebel

Here are two prayers that will help your walk towards total freedom from this power. The first prayer is about taking ownership or accountability for where we ourselves have been controlling in other people's lives.

> "In Jesus' name, I repent and renounce every place in my life where I have allowed the Jezebel spirit to operate through me, where through my own fear and rejection I have been controlling or manipulating, or where I have used any form of intimidation to achieve my own goals.
>
> I repent of not trusting you, Lord, to do the fighting for me, of pushing my own way. I repent of any place or time where I have been dominating or controlling. I ask you, Lord, to forgive me now and wash me clean as I receive your forgiveness and your grace. Thank you, Father."

Prayer to renounce the effects of Jezebel:

"In Jesus' name I renounce and break off the spirit of *fear, domination and intimidation* that has operated against me in my life. I renounce and break off the family spirit of Jezebel that has tried to rule me all my life and rule my parents, my spouse, and my children. I renounce and separate myself away from the spirit of Jezebel that has operated particularly through _____, that created fear, passivity and indecision in me and silenced my voice from speaking out. I renounce the silencing on my tongue and the inability to express my words and God's words through me.

I break the power of the lie that I have nothing to say to anyone of any interest, for the truth is that out of my innermost being shall flow rivers of living water and I shall bless with my mouth and praise the name of the Lord. In fact, I refuse to be silent. I repent of where I have been an Ahab, passive and fearful. The truth is that God did not give me a spirit of fear but of love, power and a sound mind. I speak off any fear of insanity, of dementia, of Alzheimer's disease.

I speak off the fear of dying before my time, for the truth is I shall live out my allotted years. As I honour my mother and my father everything shall go well with me and I shall live long in the land God gives me. I refuse to be a fountain sealed up, and I speak a release to my tongue to speak God's words. I loose my tongue now to speak the love of God, to speak in power and to prophesy God's words with power, authority and boldness. Ecclesiastes 3 says that there is a time to speak and a time to be silent, and I declare I will speak in the timing of God. My speech will be clear and I will bless many by my words. I remove all tentacles of Jezebellic wounding from my heart; all effects from control and domination are coming off me now.

I renounce the family iniquity of mockery, belittling and derision and in particular I forgive _____ for the words of humiliation they spoke over me. I ask you, Lord, to heal my heart as I release to you the pain from that. I declare that fear is breaking off me now, that Your perfect love casts out all fear, and I command all fear to leave me now, all anxiety and all intimidation. I rise up in all I am called to do and speak what I am to speak. Fear has no place in my life now. By the blood of Jesus and what He has accomplished on the Cross, I can now walk in total freedom without fear."

CHAPTER THIRTEEN

The Postmodern Church

Modernism to Postmodernism

Modernism	16th century to 2000
Premodern	Up to 1500
Postmodern	2000 onwards

We are now in the postmodern era, which is anything from 2000 onwards.

In late modernism the arts took a back seat, then got out of the vehicle altogether and had to hitch a ride. The arts then became entertainment for the masses. I believe, as Christians, we're usually too busy with our programs to "indulge" ourselves with allowing our creative self out for a run.

We are standing now with an antiquated, dinosaur dodo-dead church model that no longer works, and we know it. God is doing His utmost to dismantle and disable this model from working. We *must* stop hanging on to the sinking ship.

The last seven words of a church model in its death throes are, "We've never done it this way before." Indeed.

In this millennium we are moving into such change we will wonder why we stuck with the old model so long.

God is saying, "Take your heart along with you!"

In 1 Samuel 19, we see a situation of misplaced loyalty to some degree. It's about Jonathan, David and Saul. King Saul was a psychotic control freak with a major jealousy problem. At the end of his reign he was consulting witches, and all that was left of the dynasty was crippled offspring named Mephibosheth (2 Samuel 4). We often seem to have a season of serving a "Saul" leader before we find a David. We often come out from serving Saul, however, with lameness which speaks of our walk with God and blindness where we have had our spiritual sight removed.

So we find ourselves in postmodernism, and we are standing where the medieval stood when they realized the earth was not flat, feudalism was dead, and the Industrial Revolution had begun. They clung to the old models.

Unless we become a people relevant to the culture and stop separating away from it we will go nowhere.

In the church that my husband and I are a part of, the church is in the centre of the New Age culture in Australia. There are cults, counter-cults, sects, and streams hitherto unheard of. It also attracts millions of tourists from all over the world. I can assure you this church is entirely relevant to the culture it finds itself in. The leader is an apostle and his wife is a prophet and they have certainly done the hard yards in establishing a community of passionate Christian believers. We love it.

Jesus constantly sent groups *into* the culture, not to destroy it and to take the evil out but to preserve the arts within the culture. This is the missionary challenge of the third millennium. Righteousness is about arriving, representing Jesus *into* the culture, not about being disinfected from it in some sterile, germ-free bubble. Historically, missionaries from British shores and other colonies have tried to eradicate the whole cultures (e.g. Australian aborigines, Indians, Africans, Native Americans, and Maoris).

Sadly, Aboriginal art has now become entertainment. They have a deep belonging to the land, yet land rights are not about ownership but stewardship of what has been given. Their animism is idolatry; idolatry is simply esteeming something or someone to a higher place than Jesus Christ. Jesus came to *redeem* the culture not *condemn* it.

Again, historically, Christianity has often withdrawn from the culture and created its own, which is often sterile, non-productive and cloning, in which all look the same, sound the same and smell the same. In its extreme it becomes a cult, but as it is, it can simply be religiosity.

We are meant to invade the culture but not destroy it. It's not about a dress code. Respectability is not a fruit of the Spirit but often a hallmark of rigid religion, hoping to reflect on the outside what is on the inside.

I remember once doing a weekend prophetic seminar in a church in Queensland, Australia, and on Saturday all the leaders and elders wore blue jeans and chequered shirts and on Sunday they all wore cream slacks and a navy blue jacket! God is such a diverse creator, bearing colours and sounds not yet heard. Dare to be different.

As we throw ourselves into *all* our creativity, it becomes obedience rather than a sacrifice. Our postmodern theology needs to be demonstrated not just through words but also through sound, music, poetry, art, dance etc.

In other cultures where singing, narration, art and dance are indigenous to the culture, they would ask a wounded person, "When did you stop singing, etc.?" Mostly in Western culture we didn't even start!

It is a time to journey from the life we find ourselves in to the real life God has for us, full of vibrancy, colour and creativity; to connect with our true heart, the one God gave us that we keep disowning, denying and often try to kill.

We must never believe the mundane is the norm. To desire something better is to risk pain; to love again is to risk pain, but to kill desire is to kill our hearts altogether.

Our heart is our most treasured possession, so we need to guard it. Guard it for its preciousness, but not as you would a wild animal in a cage that might run rampant if it escapes. God says to us in Proverbs 4:23, *"...guard your heart with all vigilance ... for out of it flow the springs of life."* (AMP) To stop standing at the crossroads

175

and allow desire its fullness is simply frightening because we must give up controlling our life.

To not desire more in life, in God, in relationship, is to retire from life. Jesus asked constantly to those who sought Him out, "What do you want?" At least ask yourself the question too.

Don't leave your heart behind; God has promised to give us the desires in our hearts (Psalm 37:4).

In our quest to identify and then win back what has been lost along the way, I believe it is important to get an equipping mentality, a "possessing of lost and stolen ground" mentality.

Why do we equip? Because the church model in the postmodern era is not about existing as a social club for its members but about equipping the people to go out into the world. The difference is that it's a "going out" amongst all who do not yet know the love of Christ; into the market place, the corporate areas, to musicians, artists, hospital workers, the elderly and infirm, in fact wherever God is pleased to send us.

The church can become a big vacuum cleaner sucking people out of neighbourhoods so their energy can be sucked up into programmes. Jesus is not a programme or an agenda but a King who reigns in supreme majesty and wants to inhabit us. Change is coming!

I believe that the church does not exist for the benefit of its members but for the benefit of the world. The church has to become an equipping organism with many house churches being birthed by natural birth processes. Jesus *does* want His church back, and whilst He is pleased to be the guest of honour, He is also the MC. When we release Jesus to do His thing, He releases us to do more than we could ever imagine.

I see God building communities of communities, tribes joining through common ideologies and relevant theologies. I see healing communities, arts communities and places for equipping, to teach and train in life skills, prayer communities and retreats. Social skills, arts, crafts re-emerge in this model.

I see a whole house church movement re-emerging; caring groups embracing all peoples of all backgrounds; not becoming insular and introspective, turning their back on the body of Christ simply to be different, but embracing and endorsing the diversity of emerging ministries.

Even in secular space, the biggest catchword now is "community".

There can be a new postmodern type of "Bible College" that actually equips people of all ages in relevant areas such as the prophetic, the arts and the pursuit of all things bright and beautiful such as:

- Prophetic evangelism, incorporating training in "treasure hunts" (i.e. receiving words of knowledge about those who will be met on the street, then finding those people and praying for them as their treasure.)
- Sending people out to shopping malls with their prophetic evangelistic gift, to bars, service sites, sports fields, campsites, video game parlours, other churches, to observe the culture and come back and pray into it.
- Studying contemporary culture so people can relate to it.
- Having good, ongoing mentoring.
- Doing missionary healing trips into poorer countries with apostolic leadership.

This is about life-long learning, not just a three-year course. The Catholic Church has had this ideology for years with communities being established all over the world, feeding the poor, ministering into communities and changing mindsets.

The New Wineskin

God is tired of the old wineskin, and so are we. The wind of God is blowing away the denominational structures of the old model. Part of this new wineskin is about the covering of Christ Himself, and the raising up of apostolic men and women with a true father heart to love people through to maturity, to give the security of relationship from a healed heart, healed particularly of all their own father issues.

It is no good planting churches unless we are also equipping people for the work of the ministry and moving them in to healing of their addictions, pain and trauma.

This is about the saints movement – ordinary people like us, being raised up and in the hands of an extraordinary God, not "doing church" but doing in this world what we are called to do. Like the guys with Jesus, we may still smell of fish and revolution.

There are three main reforms in church history and we currently are in the third one.

1. Grace and faith, implemented by Martin Luther.
2. Intimacy, through the Moravian movement which introduced intimacy through prayer.
3. A reformation of structure.

This is about the release of the apostolic worldwide, which has been written about in previous chapters. This is the new order where churches and ministries are governed by the Father heart of God in the newly emerging apostles. This reformation will necessarily change church structure. We don't throw out anything that is real and valid; we keep the Apostles' Creed, we keep communion, we keep baptism, we don't neglect assembling together, we pray for the sick, but we stop looking at the back of people's heads. We begin training and equipping centres, confessing our sins so that we may be healed, meeting frequently simply to have friendship and relationships. We will see less programmes, committees, jumble sales and fetes, and start releasing people to go to nations.

God is turning the church upside down so that the true leaders – the apostles – are the servants of all, equipping those whom they serve. Historians now are discovering that the bishops, overseers in the Bible, were more custodians of the flock that supervisors. The early church is our prototype not our ideal.

The number of miracles, conversions and growth in Kingdom numbers already surpasses anything in the Bible's recorded history. We have asked for kings and often received Sauls. Now we have the true king and the true Kingdom, and it's time to take our place in it.

Listen! All creation is groaning.

God is releasing whole prophetic companies of people who are based on care, prayer and friendship, bonded through food. Companies that eat together as well as pray together stay together in community.

It's a time where the pastoral office is very rocky and being released in the wider sense – not removed, of course, but substantiated and endorsed in a different way. Pastors are being released to do just that: pastor and shepherd the flock God has given them. Nothing extra. The day of the true prophetic teacher is coming, where the revelation word of God will come to the teacher as a download from God. The seed bags are bursting at the seams and the ground is being made ready!

God is raising up captains and generals who will instil order but not hierarchy, who walk with a limp and who identify with Jesus in suffering, betrayal and rejection but have had their hearts healed and are envisioned and functional.

God alone qualifies the disqualified. If your life has been about falling, failing and generally stuffing up, get ready, God can't wait to use you.

Let's leave our baggage behind. I see the Lord fast-forwarding emotional healing in unprecedented ways, so that we can rise up into all God has for us to do.

Hearing comes from intimacy. Intimacy produces. And reproduces after its own kind.

God is emphasizing alignment and convergence at the moment. Alignment and convergence equal favour of God. It is vital now to be at the right place at the right time.

There is a convergence coming of ministries and people that will surprise many. It is a rallying time, therefore it is important to be correctly aligned and find your flag and your flagship.

Some people will get out of the boat they are in, to be furthered along. Some need to stay and continue to be a demonstration of Jesus. Some need to go or they won't fulfil their calling.

If you need to move and be re-positioned then it is your time to do so.

Your sphere of influence comes from the favour of God. When God wants to transform an area He raises up people and moves them. In the land of your anointing you are empowered to a higher level just because God designed it for you.

The Next Move

God is releasing a new sound in the world and, in fact, the same adulation that the Beatles had is coming back to Jesus. A lot of musicians are too bored to stay in church as they can feel too "locked in" and "programmed". However, the church is the bride of the Lord and we are called to serve the bride, whether we are received in our prophetic capacity or not. This is basic to our calling and our purpose, even though the church can be full of irritation and annoyance (as can the emerging prophetic company).

We need each other so that the sandpaper ministry can happen and our rough places can become smooth. Both the church that rejects the prophets and the prophets that reject the church can simply be about preference and wanting to stay comfortable in the familiar, but when each embraces the other, maturity can occur and God exhorts us to *"go on to maturity"* in Hebrews 6:1.

We all need to receive mercy and grace for our failures and the understanding that we don't always have to be right or in control.

Our true ministry starts at the burial site of fear of man. True humility is agreeing with who God says you are and with what He has called you to. Stop apologizing for it. Pick it up – accept it and embrace it.

False humility is knowing what God has called you to but receiving it with a "worm mentality". In Ephesians 4:1 Paul begs us *"to lead a life worthy of the calling to which you have been called with behaviour that is a credit to the summons to God's service."*

Prodigals (Lavish Squanderers of Inheritances) are Returning

The unsaved know God loves them – it's the people of God they're not sure about. Most non-Christians quite like Jesus but do not understand lordship. Religion never wants to throw a party for the "baddies", but Jesus spent 95% of His time with them. We, generally speaking, spend it with other Christians.

If you are afraid you will "backslide" by going to the world, don't go. (Luke 15:1). If we want to reach those that don't know Jesus yet, we need to change the "Christianese" language (e.g. "washed in blood" can sound like a satanic ritual!)

Don't be found as an "elder brother", resentful of grace and jealous of attention, for it is the Father's heart to restore.

This is the Elijah heart coming back through the prophets of God; the return of the prodigal sons and daughters – and we are all prodigal in relation to a true returning to the Father's heart.

This is about to happen. It is the Elijah company of prophets that ushers in this particular revival of a turning of hearts of sons and daughters to fathers, and fathers to their children. When fathers start to take accountability of where they have been lacking towards their families, something shifts in the spirit. We are currently seeing a global pandemic of fatherlessness with its outworkings on the next generation. The Father's heart is particularly expressed through the apostolic, and we are about to see a revival sparked by a return to the Father.

CHAPTER FOURTEEN

Worship, a Way of Life

Music Belongs to the Lord

We have been created as worshippers of our God. All creation worships Him. Our spirit longs to worship, and our soul and body respond to that. It is through intimacy and time spent that we get to really know someone, and God is no different. As we spend time in worship (whatever form that takes) whether it be in silence, in appreciation of beauty, in music, song, art or dance or any other of the myriads of ways to worship our beautiful King, we begin to hear His love song towards us.

If you can hear the sound of grinding these days, it is probably the church changing gears as it gears up for the revolution of new sound. The whole of creation is groaning right now: rocks, trees, oceans, and lands. In Romans 8:22 the Word talks of creation *"...moaning together in the pains of labor..."* (AMP) That's pretty dramatic stuff.

> You are worthy, our Lord and God, to receive glory and honour and power, for you created all things, and by your will they were created and have their being.
>
> *Revelation 4:11 (NIV)*

Music belongs to God. Worship is a lifestyle, not a Sunday morning exercise. It is not the warm up to the sermon. Jesus is central, not the pulpit. We must worship the Lord of the worship, not the worship of the Lord.

God is about to put himself into a new wineskin.

There is coming a re-establishment of art, drama and music in the church, which, as history shows, used to be a centre of creativity. It is all about to be about the arts, hearts and healing.

Healing that comes through the release of creativity is ancient. In indigenous cultures globally, emotional recovery has come through narration, poetry, dancing, art and singing. Mostly in Western society we never started creating. It is time now to journey from the life we find ourselves in towards the real life that God has for us, to connect with our true heart, the creative part of our spirit we were born with (you know, the one we often deny as being unimportant, unnecessary and hardly of any importance in getting the world saved).

Our Father God, the creator of all things, is practically bashing the door down, wanting to burst out of the confines that we have had Him held in, to sing, to dance, to write and whatever your spirit is drawn to do. Now that's true worship: presenting our bodies – *"all your members and faculties"* (AMP) according to Romans 12:1 – as a living sacrifice to a living God.

This year a friend gifted me with eleven fabulous art class lessons. I have been balking at this for probably fifteen years, even though as a child I would draw and paint endlessly. I was terrified of the blank canvas. As I lifted my brush for the first time, my eyes spilled over with tears and I could no longer see. It was, I feel, a combination of a fear being faced and a relief to finally be doing what I have always loved. I have always been a writer (that was easy) but a painter? I learned to shoot the censor in my head that was so critical and judgemental and told me it was not good enough, and absolutely enjoyed the whole experience. My teacher could not believe how prolific my works were and how it seemed I already had a style that gushed and flooded out of me. I just smiled and felt the smile too of my Father God. I felt like the woman in Song of Solomon 4:12 – *"a garden enclosed and barred is my sister, my [promised] bride – a spring shut up, a fountain sealed"* – being suddenly unstopped and unstoppable.

True Worshippers

To celebrate in worship together is to worship in spirit and in truth (John 4:24). We don't so much *go* to church; we *are* the church.

A stage represents performing. God wants to close the gap between the stage and the people. The great gulf between the laity and the clergy; the whole "us and them" situation which needs to close and converge. I am looking forward to the day when we can share our resources across churches, across cities and regions, where if a small struggling church needs a couple of guitarists and a worship leader we can serve across the board. This is an understanding of the stewardship of the Kingdom and not ownership of resources and people.

Worship is about attitude, determining altitude, and leads to clarity of hearing. We so need His breath to breathe on us and revive our dry bones. Satan may be the prince of the power of the air, but we change that through our worship. It is not the warm up before the service; it *is* our service (Romans 12:1). Our "service" and worship are the dedication of our lives to God. The pulpit is not the centre; the throne room of Jesus is.

Tobiah's Room

In Nehemiah 13:5 we read that Tobiah had been given a room by Eliashib, to whom he was related by marriage. Tobiah had basically moved into the areas set aside to store the grain and the oil which was part of the provision given to the Levites, the delegated singers and musicians who implemented twenty-four hour worship 365 days a year for thirty-three years (2 Chronicles 5).

Originally the Levitical priesthood, the musicians and singers were given a part of the offering, along with the priest.

But exactly who was Tobiah? He had wormed himself in with the leadership politically and by marriage, but was unable to prove he had any connection with Israel. He had been given space in the house of God. It was a place that belonged to God's prophetic musicians and singers. All had gone back to earning a living, but God restored their position through Nehemiah's action of throwing out Tobiah's household goods (a bit like Jesus overthrowing the market stalls in the temple) and cleansing the space again, restoring the Levites to bring worship to the house of God.

Many musicians are being hidden by God at the moment and will emerge in the fullness of time, the timing of God. Many, too, have been taken captive by the adulation of the world or by their own excesses, and like the psalmists and musicians who were taken into Babylon, they hung their harps up on the willow trees in lamentation and longing for their own land. There are too many harps on too many willows. Many musicians are sitting down in Babylon weeping and mourning over remembrance of their mountaintop experience as a worshipping muso, before the control came, before that sin in their life caused them to really fall and there was no one to restore.

The "Joshua Generation" is not so much about young people but it is a remnant of mature leaders released to bring young ones out. This is the release of the apostolic Father's heart. This is the release of the healing prophets, the Elijah company that will turn the hearts of children and fathers and point them to God.

The day of Psalmody is not finished. In the book of Acts, when heaven came to earth as the mob was assembled in the upper room, it was a *sound* – not the wind itself but the sound of it. The early church was birthed through sound. In the Garden of Eden, Adam and Eve heard the sound of God in the garden. What did He sound like? He is depicted variously in the Bible as the sound of rushing wind, as water, and as fire. All three components carry sound and all that sound is in God.

In Hebrews 1:7 it speaks of God making His angels winds and his servants flames of fire. Even rocks can carry sound, and Jesus talks about the very rocks crying out in worship. God is always releasing a new sound, a new song, a song like no other. The mundane is not the norm. Look for more because it is here.

Pitfalls for Singers and Musicians

JEALOUSY AND ENVY:

Jealousy can consume a person, particularly one who is insecure about their identity. It is actually about lack of trust. It is guarding the little we think we own, for fear of losing it. Jealousy says, "I am not satisfied with the little bit God has given me. I can't trust Him to build on it in His own way and time. I want what that person has. I covet their gift." Envy is a little different in that it is a deep, resentful desire for what someone else has, without recognizing the gift that God has already given.

IDOLATRY:

Idolatry is placing anything or anyone – a ministry, a gift, a relationship – in the place that belongs to the lordship of Jesus. Musicians, if you have anointing on what you do, you may have a "following". The danger is that people may seek the gift rather than the giver of it, which can be idolatry. Idolatry occurs whenever we give to creation what belongs to the creator – God. The Lord often has to pull down what we have built, to build what He wants. The devil builds us particularly as musicians and singers only to destroy us. God will allow us to go through wilderness years to build His character so He can trust us to carry the anointing. We need to learn to die quietly and with dignity.

SELFISH AMBITION:

We are called to serve the King, our Lord Jesus, first and foremost. True service rests in the hiddenness of contented obscurity for however long God says. Self-denial means I don't have to control and manipulate everything and have my own way. Learn to play to an audience of one person: Jesus.

PERFORMANCE:

The word performance means "to be extraordinary beyond human strength". If you need feedback because of your own insecurities, practice in empty rooms and blank walls, ocean shores and woodlands until you reach the heart of God. "Worship" means to lick hand, like an adoring dog. To worship is "to kiss towards the Son".

AVOIDING QUARRELS:

We have one enemy and it is not each other. We all know the trap of the intensity of a potential argument between spouses /friends/families on the way to church or similar. Be aware of strategies to disarm you before you play/sing. What triggers you? Face it. Recognize it. War against it. Carry the treasure. Try to not get caught up with other people's baggage just before you minister. Don't forget the simple things like getting enough sleep and rest.

DISCERNING THE ANOINTING:

The anointing of the Holy Spirit is unpredictable. It can cause tears, sobs or laughter. The outward manifestation can be an indication of inward change. Mercy comes at point of need.

Sometimes it is not so much an actual manifestation of the Holy Spirit but the *effect* of the Holy Spirit touching something – an emotion, a memory, a wound or the spirit of a person.

God shook a whole mountain. Who are we to resist what God will do? God's intensity is increasing. He wants to have intimacy with us, to be face to face and eye to eye.

> On the morning of the third day there was thunder and lightning, with a thick cloud over the mountain, and a very loud trumpet blast ... the LORD descended ... in fire. The smoke billowed up ... like smoke from a furnace, and the whole mountain trembled violently.
>
> *Exodus 19:16,18 (NIV)*

187

Wow! That is God.

Jesus says, *"Come up here, and I will show you..."* (Revelation 4:1, AMP).

Early Music History

The first recorded musician was Jubal (Genesis 4:21). He was the *"father of all those who {played} the lyre and pipe"* (AMP).

The first recorded praise was Genesis 4:26: *"...At that time men began to call {praise, intercede} the name of the Lord."* (AMP) This was the time of Seth's son, Enosh. Seth's line established a true dependency on the Lord.

Levi was Leah and Jacob's third son (Genesis 29:34), the original ancestor of the Israeli priests. His character was savage and merciless, but we need this for warfare intercession.

Levites were known as instruments of wrath, which is the true heart of the intercessor – anger at the enemy. It is also the true heart of musicians and singers in warfare; we are spiritual "hit men". The Levites were put together as a team of battling worshippers. They worshipped twenty-four hours a day, for thirty-three years (i.e. one full day for every day Jesus walked on earth). Four thousand of them worshipped. When Israel was exiled, the Levites disappeared and stopped worshipping (Ezekiel 44:10).

Musical sound is made by the vibration of moving air. Interestingly, one of the titles of Satan is *"prince of the power of the air"*. Music is a language of the spirit, from "Muse" meaning "to think about". God calls us his poems.

In Ezekiel 28:13 it speaks of Satan originally being music; the reeds, tabrets and pipes were built *into* him as the breath of God blew through in music. Through every precious stone in his garments the glory of God was reflected. The very universe was put together and created to an accompaniment of the greatest orchestra ever assembled. Job 38:7 says, *"...while the morning stars sang together and all the sons of God shouted for joy..."* (AMP)

"Lucifer" literally means "light bringer". When God said, "Let there be light," sound came forth.

Satan's Old Job

Worship leaders, or *"chief musicians"*, have Satan's old job: to cover the throne of God with continual adoration and worship. He was called "the covering cherub" in Ezekiel 28. The devil tries every strategy known to keep God's prophetic musicians out of the church; unhealed, wounded and addicted to anything and everything. He will always fear what we can become when we know our true identity. He will always mock what he fears.

We are called to worship with all of heaven and fill the airwaves with the vibration of the sound of worship. We worship Jesus for His worth and preciousness

Formation of the Choir

In 1 Chronicles 15:16,22,28, David instructs the leaders of the Levites to elect the chief musician. Today we would call him the main worship leader. Various musicians with their instruments were appointed to do nothing but worship God. Kenaniah was the head Levite and in verse 22 it says he *"was put in charge of carrying the ark and lifting up song. He instructed about these matters because he was skilled and able."* (AMP) He trained the Levites for seven to fifteen years.

THE LEVITES:

- They had an amazing understanding of poetry.
- They were full of the word of God.
- They built their own instruments from special wood, and saw them as an extension of themselves.
- They were under their father's supervision, and had good respect for authority.

> Only to the tribe of Levi Moses gave no inheritance; the sacrifices ... to the Lord, the God of Israel, are their inheritance.
>
> *Joshua 13:14 (AMP)*

> ...for the priesthood of the Lord is their inheritance.
>
> *Joshua 18:7 (AMP)*

God has created all music, so we inherit it as ours as His children. Instruments, chords and music are not demonically inspired, only people are.

King David knew great anointing and great forgiveness. He knew the mercy of God, and God loved his *"broken and ... contrite heart"* (Psalm 51:17, AMP).

Tabernacle of David

God is restoring the simple tent of David (Acts 55:16) where David and Levites sang *by revelation* to the Lord. This is intimacy between God and man, where we are called the friends of God; where Jesus has opened a permanent door of access of face to face communion, *"...to gaze upon the beauty ... of the Lord."* (Psalm 27:4, AMP)

What attracts the Holy Spirit to a gathering of believers? Always worship. Surely, we do not want to repeat the mistakes from the past?

The Key of David

> ...these are the words of the Holy One, the True One, <u>He Who has the key of David, Who opens and no one shall shut, Who shuts and no one shall open</u>...
>
> *Revelation 3:7 (AMP, emphasis added)*

> I will place on his shoulders the key to the house of David; what he opens no one can shut, and what he shuts no one can open.
>
> *Isaiah 22:22 (NIV)*

The *Key of David* is the hand of the Lord in worship, extended to His psalmists to open the door to heaven so we can bring others up to and through, in worship.

The door that is closed is the door to religion, flesh, hype and the counterfeit intrusion of Satan. Satan hates prophetic worshippers and psalmists because of their ability to open the doors of heaven to flood the church with prophetic worship. This is where God loves to come and His glory will be manifested.

If we can worship God in spirit and in truth, we can also do it in the flesh and in lies. We need to be honest and transparent about our failings. There may be a hundred things wrong with us but usually God in His kindness and mercy only deals with us one thing at a time. Thank God for God!

Worship creates an atmosphere where we can hear the voice of God very clearly and receive instruction, reproof, healing and encouragement. A heart of gratitude is an essential ingredient to worshipping in truth.

Beholding His Face

> I saw heaven standing open and there before me was a white horse, whose rider is called Faithful and True.
>
> *Revelation 19:11 (NIV)*

Our worship opens up the Heavenly realm, with God inhabiting our praises and angels joining in with us.

Revelation 1:13 describes His robe, His head, His hair, His feet, His eyes, His voice, His mouth and His face. Isaiah 6:1 says, *"I saw the Lord, sitting upon a throne, high and lifted up, and the skirts of His train filled the [most holy part of the] temple."* (AMP) Isaiah continues in verse 4, saying, *"At the sound of their voices the doorposts and thresholds shook and the temple was filled with smoke."* (NIV) That is a whole lot of shaking!

Summary of Strategies the Enemy Uses Against Musicians

FALSE HUMILITY:

"I am only a worm and worthless." Don't hide your talents; produce more. Embrace your call, don't run from it. Pick up what God hands you. It is yours.

PRIDE:

"I am too good for the body of Jesus. I'll get famous first, then I'll play." Pride is revealed by the need to perform and show myself, the need for recognition by people, the need for title, and the need of feeling important. Pride comes from a base of rejection.

REJECTION:

Having a grasshopper mentality (i.e. "I deserve nothing.")
We *are* no match for the devil – *God* is. "I'll get my Dad." *He* has crushed the devil's head with his holy heel. He has ripped out his lying throat, but uses us to implement the victory won.
We need to sing out what's in God's heart today. God wants us to draw from the full well inside us and sing spontaneous worship to Him.

> The level of intimacy will rise when we go beyond the familiar to sing spontaneous expressions to him.

Intimacy costs us. When God rips the veil it is painful to see ourselves like Isaiah did when he said, *"Woe is me! ... I am a man of unclean lips..."* Isaiah also said, *"In the year that King Uzziah died, [in a vision] I saw the Lord..."* Sometimes it takes the death of a thing, idol, ministry, person to *see* the Lord (Isaiah 6:1-8, AMP).

There is a difference between memorized lines and the spontaneous (e.g. at a wedding, "I promise to love, honour and obey..." etc.) It makes no sense to keep repeating the same pre-composed words once the heart wants to love. Write new psalms today. God is calling us as psalmists to describe with a new language of love His mercies, wisdom and love to us. He longs to hear us.

Psalming

Definition: "It is the creating of words and melody under the anointing of the Holy Spirit, singing prophetically the song of the Lord."

Anyone may "psalm", but the anointing is stronger when it comes through a prophet or prophetic person. The day of Psalmody is being released to greater heights, to release the glory of God across nations everywhere. When we open the gates of righteousness, they are too heavy to open alone and it takes a team. God is building worshipping communities to open up the gates collectively, teams that are like what is mentioned in Joel:

> They run like mighty men; they climb the wall like men of war. They march each one ... on his ways, and they do not break their ranks. Neither does one thrust another; they walk every one in his path. And they burst through and upon the weapons, yet they are not wounded and do not change their course. The earth quakes before them; the heavens tremble...
>
> *Joel 2:7-10 (AMP)*

Psalmists have learned to minister to God alone out in the back blocks of the wilderness and now sing to their King from a place of brokenness and contriteness. In Psalm 42, David, the psalmist, expresses passion and longing for the Lord, exhorting his soul to rise up and not be depressed, that his hope is in the living God. The psalms are full of the realness of pain, depression, overwhelming grief and disappointment.

Scanning

This is what I call the art of listening to God for words of knowledge, discerning of spirits, visions, prophetic words, changes in the anointing, such as warfare, healing release, while still playing

193

or singing, and generally looking to God for where He wants to take the music on a particular occasion.

It is the ability, and in fact the necessity, of throwing out the programme, the list, the service order and going with the Holy Spirit who actually *knows* which way to go.

The psalmist, who can be the chief musician or worship leader, can receive a word of wisdom, knowledge, healing release or prophecy for the whole congregation or simply individuals. We must move beyond concentration of playing and singing into a dimension in the spirit to hear what the Spirit is saying to the church. We become as a blind pianist, tuning in to the voice of God for the people. We can pierce through the heavenlies with one note of voice or instrument to bring healing or deliverance to people. We can impart to people as they are in an anointing of worship so they can release hurts, wounds, forgiveness or conviction of sin. God has a sneaky way of unzipping us and breaking and entering our hearts to perform love surgery.

Times of Selah

Many times in the psalms it is written, "selah," which means to stop our frenzied activity, pause, and think about whatever was just said or written. These are the times when all is quiet and we calmly consider God and His mercy towards us etc. It provides opportunity to repent, to be healed of our wounds. It is a time to scan and see in the spirit which direction on this particular journey to go. This is a time to let a new song begin amongst the singers, let the musicians "go for it". It is like sailing into uncharted waters with only the stars to guide you.

This can, however, be the time when frightened leadership says, "Let's all be seated now and read the newsletter," and God was about to descend with a shout and take us all away to the mountaintop! This is immensely frustrating for true worshippers, who adore the freedom of the wild heart of Jesus. Because we are all flesh *and* spirit *and* soul, in a worship band or group of singers some parts of each will be present at any given time.

It is worth the risk to hear from the heart of God; you can always fix it up later on.

Minstrels

> But now, bring me a minstrel. And while the minstrel played, the hand and power of the Lord came upon [Elisha].
>
> *2 Kings 3:15 (AMP)*

When I first started out with trembling little steps into prophetic ministry, I found my way into the joy of psalming and singing prophetically over people. The song of the Lord simply grabs the person you are singing over, connecting their heart with the heart of the loving Father. We become then the downloading mechanism, or hosepipe for God to flow down. I needed a minstrel to effectively back this up, and many times my son Josh would accompany me as I ministered.

In 1 Samuel 16:14,23, we read how Saul was delivered from an evil spirit through a psalmist (David) singing. The minstrel anointing is a horizontal as well as a vertical one; it releases a prophetic anointing to enable another to prophesy. It is much easier to prophesy with a sensitive prophetic minstrel playing as you do it; you can ride your anointing on top of his. We can have a minstrel play as we preach, as we minister as a prayer team in healing and restoration, in deliverance etc. Like the piano player at the movies when the silent movies began so we can provide an emphasis to the Word as it is preached.

Prophetic Song and the Song of the Lord

The "song of the Lord" is the spirit of prophecy expressing the heart of God, the thoughts and intentions of God through song. It is Jesus singing. *"He will exult over {us} with singing"* (Zephaniah 3:17, AMP).

195

Beyond Prophetic

This is when the spirit of prophesy touches a person with a special anointing to sing a song of love, of war, of edification or exhortation to the rest of the church, expressing the heart of God to the people.

WHAT IS IT FOR? WHOM IS IT TO?

- A song towards the Lord (e.g. Mary's song, in Luke 1:46: *"My soul magnifies and extols the Lord."* AMP)
- A song sung over a person, bringing release, encouragement and comfort and healing.
- To the Bridegroom from the bride, as a love song (e.g. Song of Soloman 5:10: *"My beloved is fair {and} chief among ten thousand!"* AMP)
- A song of war directed at *the enemy* (e.g. Psalm 60:12: *"Through God we shall do valiantly, for it is He who shall tread down our adversaries."* AMP)

SCRIPTURAL SUPPORT FOR THE SONG OF THE LORD

> Then some Levites ... stood up and praiseed the Lord ... with a very loud voice ... Jehoshophat appointed men to sing to the Lord and to praise Him for the splendour of his holiness ... As they began to sing and praise, the Lord set ambushes against the men ... who were invading Judah...
>
> *2 Chronicles 20:19,21-22*

When prophecy is sung, it carries a huge impact to the hearers, depending on the authority of the one who is singing. Authority released is often seen by weak and jealous people as pride.

The Psalms are full of allusions to "a new song". This is the song of the Lord, fresh from the throne of God to build up, enrich and edify the people. It is our "manna".

In Revelation 14:3 we read that in heaven *"they sung a new song before the throne..."*

Sing to yourselves psalms, hymns, spiritual songs, making melody to the Lord.

Ephesians 5:19 (NIV)

There can be a corporate anointing of a spirit of prophecy in a group of people and then *all may prophesy*, either in song or speech. The song of the Lord broke out when the Israelites had crossed successfully from Egypt. In Exodus 15:1-3, we read how Moses the prophet sang the song of the Lord: *"I will sing to the Lord, for He has triumphed gloriously; the horse and its rider or its chariot, has He thrown into the sea. The Lord is my Strength and my Song and He has become my Salvation; this is my God and I will praise Him, my father's God and I will exalt Him. The Lord is a Man of War, The Lord is His name."* (AMP) Miriam the prophetess (verse 20) took a timbrel in her hand, and all the women went after her with timbrels and dancing singing, *"Sing to the Lord for He has triumphed gloriously..."* (verse 21, NIV).

Prophetic Declaration

This is where we declare prophetically, either in song or speech, the word of God into a situation or a person's life (e.g. *"Your kingdom come, your will be done..."* – Matthew 6:10, NIV). We can declare light, healing, restoration, joy or any other positive declaration from the word of God. The world was declared into being prophetically in the beginning (Genesis 1).

WHY USE IT?

Prophetic declaration can be used as a result of having sought the Lord in prayer for words of knowledge, words of wisdom, and a prophetic senses/knowledge about a situation, a region, a nation, or a person. It is used to break the negative spirit powers around a building, a church, a life or a situation.

Through [our] God we shall do valiantly...

Psalm 108:13 (AMP)

197

As we boldly declare prophetically, it changes the spirit realm in a place.

We can speak or sing God's rule into the situation (e.g. "Every knee shall bow and every tongue confess.") We are to speak the things that are not as though they are (e.g. "Your Kingdom come, your will be done.")

Prophetic declaration can expose demonic power and dethrone principalities and powers. To declare that Jesus died but rose again and is Lord of Lords *is* to declare war in the spirit realm (e.g. "The God of peace crushes Satan under His feet.")

As we declare prophetically who Jesus is, the enemy backs off (e.g. "My God is a consuming fire," "He is a God of faithfulness without injustice...")

> The Lord is my Strength and my Song, and He has become my Salvation ... The Lord is a Man of War; the Lord is His name.
>
> *Exodus 15:2-3 (AMP)*

This is a song of war – a song of victory.

May God *never* say of us: *"These people come near to me with their mouth and honour me with their lips, but their heart is far from me. Their worship is made up only of rules taught by men, learned by repetition without any thought of the meaning."* (Isaiah 29:13, NIV).

Lamentation Worship

Lamentation worship is worshipping God even though our world is in pieces. It is depicted in Habakkuk 3:17, where he says, "Even though all this dreadful calamity is happening, yet I will rejoice in the Lord, who never changes." It is celebration of the character of God, a demonstration of standing at rest in the midst of trouble. It is standing in the chasm between "though" and "yet".

A lament is sorrow expressed as an audible expression of grief. It is real and it is honest, and it is definitely not pretend happy-clappy noise with hype. It is knowledge deep in our hearts that all things are working together for our good.

Singing Intercession ("Tepillah")

David sang his petitions to God with the psalmists. The Hebrew word "Tepillah" means "to intercede and sing your prayers to God as worship". This word is used when Jesus says, *"My house shall be a house of prayer (Tepillah)"*. It is an ancient practice to sing our prayers, but very powerful.

Gregorian chants were sung by priests as an *a capella* act of worship to God. We may sing our prayers against the enemies of our families, such as rebellion, lust running wild, our teenagers being lost, and demand in prayer to have them back from the land of the enemy. This is worship and intercession being used as one weapon together, a "double whammy".

The enemy's strategy is to not just to kill you, but also destroy all that is good in and around you. He uses intimidation and fear, inferiority, accusation, passivity, lure of performance, shame, offence etc. He likes to take something or someone and make them nothing. He seems to select the people with the greatest talents and abilities and sends missiles and assignments to annihilate, if possible.

Prophetic Warfare in Music

THE NATURE OF SATAN

John 10:10 reveals that, *"The [enemy] comes only to steal and kill and destroy."* (AMP) In Isaiah 45:1-2 Jesus promises to *"unarm and ungird the loins of kings ... I will break in pieces the doors of bronze and cut asunder the bars of iron."* (AMP)

We are called as an offence to the Kingdom of darkness, but it is not a fleshly, carnal war.

> The weapons of our warfare are not physical ... but they are mighty...
>
> *2 Corinthians 10:3-4 (AMP)*

Satan hates all areas of health, unity, kindness and peace, and his habitation is every place of disunity, death, sickness, poverty and confusion. He loves to injure, disappoint and intimidate. He loves to wound, isolate and encourage hatred, and to promote rejection, misrepresentation and isolation. When he whispers lies in your ear about your littleness and inadequacy, to some degree you can agree with him because it is only "through our God we do valiantly"! We will overcome evil with good.

> ...for that enemy of yours, the devil, roams around like a lion roaring ... seeking someone to ... devour.
>
> *1 Peter 5:8 (AMP)*

PROPHETIC WARFARE

If we use every plan and purpose of the enemy to bring us into the presence of God, to give thanks in all circumstances to the Greater One, we will frustrate and confuse the demonic forces that come against us.

The devil wants you to either have no confidence in God's ability or too much in your own. He wants you to see your unredeemed self through his eyes; not the sanctified, washed clean, white-robed self, loved forever by Jesus. As we take every thought captive to Christ, turn every lustful thought to a prayer of purity, every hateful thought to a blessing, we begin to have the *"mind of Christ"* because God's whole purpose is to make us like Jesus.

> This is the man I will look to, he who is humble and contrite and trembles at my Word.
>
> *Isaiah 66:2 (NIV)*

When pride is destroyed in us, meekness, humility and transparency can come.

Victory begins with the Name of Jesus, but is not won until His nature is produced in our hearts. Victory is won in the battlefield of minds. One of the greatest lies is, we will never be ready or good enough. In our weakness, when we put the enemy to flight, it is embarrassing to him because we are in so much weakness but well able to overcome. We put one thousand to flight. Hear his footsteps fleeing!

We put out the darkness by turning on the light. It is less about looking for the enemy activity and more about preparing a way for the King with a straight path.

God is looking for true worshippers who will worship Him *"in spirit and in truth"* (John 4:23, AMP). This means, "Be real!"

AN INCREASE OF WAR

Prophetic musicians and singers are frontline warriors, and get shot at the most.

Some of God's worshippers that are in the church now are bored, tired, burnt out, and don't know what else to do but stay on out of fear, habit and exhaustion. They are often sick of the god of performance with its enormous perfectionist demands, and like circus lions who have lost their roar, they have come to accept three meals a day (the Sunday morning gig), but where God's anointing cannot flow freely, they quickly feel like the hireling rather than the son in the house.

God's prophetic worshippers need to be positioned correctly, not in religion but in pure, holy fire, set ablaze with passionate love for Jesus and hatred for evil.

A bunch of worshipping musicians *can* bring down giants; all they need is to be teachable, available and faithful.

Prophetic worship/warfare is when our "sound" becomes the voice of God to the people. The Hebrew word "rua" means "to split the ear". This is the shout of God. When our shout joins with the shout of God, walls begin to fall in people's lives.

A new foundation is coming to us: deep calling to deep, thunder from depths, becoming solid as rocks. God is restoring worship, warfare and intercession through music in the body of Christ now. It is not a season but a strategy, to bring down the giants in our own lives and others'.

The Body of Christ needs to be equipped by prophetic, apostolic leaders who walk in five-fold ministry to teach, train and equip saints for the work of ministry, to get out there and bring in the lost and hopeless, then go out and do the same again. We need worship leaders who know they are actually chief musicians, with companies of musicians who are free enough to not need to perform.

We need prophetic preachers who are free enough not to preach if God says not to. This next move is dependent on God bringing the greatest anointing of warfare/worship the church has ever seen. It takes more faith sometimes to follow the man/woman with vision than to *be* the man/ woman with the vision. Often the opposition comes from within ranks.

The new sound coming from the mountain will draw prophetic warrior musicians from every cave; and to every boring, religious institution that wants to stay within the program, God is saying, "Let my prophetic musicians *go!* Let them express their passion to Me."

The Function and Purpose of Prophetic Worshippers

Today's prophetic musicians and worshippers have not come from palaces and places of grandeur but their long preparation time has been in the cave of Adullam with their King.

They have been in the desert, in the wilderness, invisible, forgotten seemingly by everyone, hidden away under the shadow of the Almighty, being prepared for such a time as *this!*

They have learnt to be hand-fed by the ravens, nurtured on little, and when they come out people will say, " *'Who is this one, leaning on the arm of their Beloved'* and not on the arm of flesh?"

Today's prophetic musicians and worshippers simply want to worship at His feet, and want no claim, no fame, no name; and they desire that God gets all the glory.

They have allowed Him to burn His seal into their spirit, to ravish their heart; they have allowed Him to mould them on the potter's wheel and have His perfect way. They know rejection, the trashing of their reputation; their behaviour has been labelled as rebellion, as they resist control and conditioning, for it destroys their anointing.

They have become vagabonds in the spirit, following the King to the ends of the earth on a quest for freedom in worship and in ministry; they have suffered abuse of every form, misunderstanding, slander and gossip and accusation, but keep coming back to the King's embrace of love and restoration.

These prophetic ministers have no dependency on manmade institutions or doctrines; they are God-appointed and their gift makes room for them.

What man promotes, man can demote; what God appoints, remains.

Prophetic musicians and worshippers "see" with the eye of the spirit, God's eye. They *are* His senses; they sniff out Jezebel and religion. They hear and then become the trumpet voice to battle, feel and sense His total love and acceptance for the people, taste the sweetness of His wine, sing His voice and play the strings of the heart of Jesus.

Repentance

Repentance floods every part of the life of this company of prophetic musician-warriors; they literally are preparing the way of the Lord with music and song. Many of them carry a strong healing anointing and they cry, "Repent," and because of this, God's anointing is on all they do. This is the John the Baptist anointing of Malachi 4, where it speaks of turning the hearts of children and fathers to each other.

Performance Orientation

The feedback from performance will lift you out of yourself, but also out of God's anointing and into yours; it cannot belong in the heart of a worshipper. Those that have allowed performance mentality to die will play before six or six hundred because they have played to an audience of One. The King Himself has requested their presence before His throne of Grace and Mercy. We die to this part of our flesh by playing to the empty wall and not to the people.

> Performance is relying on our own ability, but when we trust God's anointing to take us, we rely solely on God. The anointing is unpredictable. It leaves you sobbing, weeping, laughing, as we sense our Father's presence.

The pursuit of excellence has been allowed to die with true worshippers, and been replaced by the pursuit of His heart.

> As the deer pants for streams of water, so my soul pants for you, O God.
>
> *Psalm 42:1 (NIV)*

Nothing else really matters to the prophetic worshipper but the pleasure of the King and His desires.

The company of prophetic worshippers and psalmists that God is raising up simply want to worship; they are sick of committees, structure, religion, ritual, "four fast songs, two slow ones", interruptions for the newsletter reading etc. Any break in the anointing of His presence is as ice water on the fire of the passion He is burning in us.

We *long* for Him with a fervency that outruns all else in our life; we just want to "hang" with the King.

God has chosen those ones who have been despised and rejected, as He was; the foolish and unexpected ones, those that have been poor in spirit and in earthly success. These ones are being brought from the back to the front and lifted up as trophies of His grace, despite everything.

God is healing them and restoring them as they bask in His warmth, kissing them to wellness with gentle words of healing and identity, and putting a fervent hatred of all evil as they declare *war* on all the enemies of the cross and allow Him to put them in Holy battle array. They allow Him to *roar* as the Lion of Judah through them and shout the battle cry, "Thus far and *no more!*"

As they take back ground now for themselves, their tribes and others, God increases their strength and their numbers and says, "Behold my mighty ones in whom I have deposited my glory!"

Selfish Ambition

God's prophetic worshippers have allowed ambition to die on the altar of humility. It becomes an idol unless we shoot it, because it draws the people to you instead of to God. Chiselled by trial, God's prophetic worshippers have allowed Him access to their hearts, allowing man to choose others over them. They wait for the King's calling and commission, content to be overlooked and seemingly forgotten as more charismatic personalities are pushed to the centre stage while they wait in the wings for the Master's voice.

Prophetic worshippers goad, stimulate, exhort, prod, awaken from passivity and comatose states, and often have to offend the mind to reveal the heart.

Our gift will make room for us as we see that we are to be allowed to let Jesus sing and play through us, even whole nights of prophetic worship, psalming and exhortation.

Twenty-four hour worship, like the Levitical Priesthood, is now returning. Hunger is returning. Longing draws the Holy Spirit.

Prophets *are* the gift of Jesus, the prophet to the church, so prophetic worshippers need a time and space to express His heart to the people, to get in amongst them and impart life to the people, and take as long as it takes.

Prophetic worshippers actually release the exact anointing required at any particular time, even during the ministry of the Word. We need to be freed up enough as leaders to worship at any time, or not at all.

We need to be non-competitive, but desire to minister alongside other five-fold misters. We refuse offence, competition, selfish ambition, performance and religious ritual.

Satan always mocks what he fears. He fears a soul sold out to God and coming into the true understanding of who he/she is called to be. He tried to kill us in the wilderness but we're back, albeit with a limp.

Satan always brings persecution to prophetic ministry because we proclaim his end and announce our King's imminent return. Remember, *"Surely the Sovereign Lord does nothing without revealing His plan to His servants the prophets."* (Amos 3:7, NIV). Satan loves respectable, "going nowhere" churches that cater to the dictates of the religious people. He likes Pharisaical, critical, dead, passive churches.

We need to be delivered from the religious expectation of man and brought into the prophetic liberty of Jesus the psalming prophet who loves to sing and play in his church.

A New Intensity of Warfare Worship

Warfare intensity is increasing, but so is intimacy, as we focus on the pure majesty of our God and King, Jesus Christ. When we realize that we are seated with Him in the heavenlies, looking down on whatever comes against us, we can begin from a place of peace and rest. We worship the King who has accomplished it all, and as we focus on the eyes of the Lord, the enemy flees.

> Let the high praises of God be in their throat and a two-edged sword in their hand; to execute vengeance upon the heathen and punishment on the people, to bind their kings with fetters, and their nobles with shackles of iron...
>
> *Psalm 149:6-9 (NIV)*

We *are* the arrows of his bow, so we get *in* the quiver; God knows where to shoot you, where to land you. Our enemies are God's enemies. We *are* a flurry of fire against them as we use our instruments and our voices!

God wants us to draw from a full well inside us and sing spontaneous worship to Him. There is a difference between memorized lines and spontaneous song. God is calling us as psalmists to describe with a new language of love His mercies, wisdom and love to us. He waits to hear us.

Biblical Examples of Radical Worship

In 2 Samuel 6:20 we see how Michal despised the radical, extravagant high praise of her husband and paid the price by never reproducing.

In Luke 19:40, when Jesus rode into Jerusalem, they ripped up the landscaped gardens and tore off their outer garments for Him to walk on. Jesus said, when asked by the religious leaders to keep the people under control (they wanted a nice orderly religious procession with an order of service and a program), *"If they keep quiet the stones will cry out"* (literally, "scream, shriek")!

Tabernacle of David

God is restoring the simple tent of David (Acts 15:16) where David and Levites sang by revelation to the Lord. This is intimacy between God and man, where we are called the friends of God. It is a forerunner to the actual time where Jesus has opened a permanent door of access of face-to-face communion.

> One thing I ask from the LORD, this only do I seek: that I may dwell in the house of the LORD all the days of my life, to gaze on the beauty of the LORD and to seek him in his temple.
>
> *Psalm 27:4 (NIV)*

The Weapons of our Warfare

- Shouting: Hebrew "ruwa", meaning "to split the ear with sound" (Psalm 47:6,7; Joshua 6:20; 2 Chronicles 15:14; Psalm 47:1; Psalm 95:1; Psalm 100:1).
- Clapping: Hebrew "taga", meaning "to strike, to drive a nail in" (Psalm 47:1, Isaiah 55:12).
- Dancing: (Psalm 150:4, 2 Samuel 6:14, Exodus 15:20).

- <u>Banners and flags</u> (Psalm 20:5, Song of Solomon 6:4,10).

A Different Warfare

Whether we are called as Levitical priests, or rank and file soldiers, our greatest warfare is a demonstration of our lives sold out to the purposes of Jesus.

> True spiritual warfare is not about noise and action alone, but it is moving in the anointing of the Holy Spirit in direct opposition to what demonic forces are dictating to you. There's a rumbling, a thundering in the prophetic warfare – worshippers who are getting free from oppression and can shout down a wall.

Acts of Warfare

In returning to Me and resting in Me you shall be saved; in quietness and confidence shall be your strength.

Isaiah 30:15 (NIV)

As we practise staying in the rest of God while the storm rages, peace comes, maturity comes. We must learn to inhabit the *"secret place of the Most High"* (Psalm 91:1), not just visit in emergencies. As we concentrate more on the hugeness of the majesty of God, the attempts from the enemy to blind and confuse and terrify will disappear. This is warring from a base of peace and of obedience.

All demonic attack is to demonstrate the power of God and bring breakthrough. We cannot war in areas where we have no effective authority. Every area you are compromising in is hidden stuff for Satan to feed on. He only has access to what we hide in the dark. Like photos, he develops our negatives in a dark place.

Our giving extravagantly in obedience is an act of warfare. Our worship to Jesus, our patience in God as we wait with no anxiety, is an act of warfare.

Forgiveness, mercy, love instead of hate, every place that we come in the opposite spirit, all are acts of war.

When we come determined to "dwell in unity" the Lord commands a blessing; this is warfare against the accuser of the brethren who uses us against each other to cause division. Husbands and wives loving each other, children obeying parents, these are acts of warfare.

Humility causes us to hide in the side of Christ and be hidden in that secret place. When the enemy comes slanging after you, he can't find you as you are hidden. The strength of humility is that it builds a defence around our soul because we realize who and whose we are.

A Declaration of Who I Am in God

"I am a prophetic warrior chosen by the King to represent Him in this time. I am a trophy of His grace; I die to pride, lay down my self-seeking ways, lay down fault-finding and a critical spirit. I speak off every cloak of shame now; my worth is in Jesus; my righteousness is in His righteousness. I break every covenant with the devil of making a silent truce, where I have said, 'You don't bother me, and I won't bother you.' I will move in my anointing in music and worship. I will sing out a new song to the Lord. I will take every inch of ground back from the enemy where it has affected me and my family, my children and my grandchildren. I will walk in the fullness of God in Jesus' name."

Find your gift. Find your place in the scheme of things. God watches over His Word to perform it, and is well able to perform it through you. Take up the challenge of this incredible time we find ourselves in. It's the best of times and the worst of times; but we can, actually, make a difference. Be as radical as God requires you to be. Waste yourself on the King and His Kingdom. He is worth it all.

Related Books by the Author

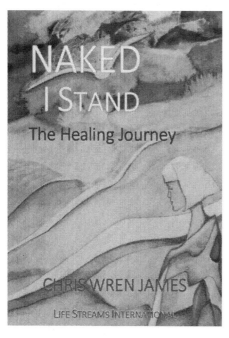

Naked I Stand
The Healing Journey

ISBN: 9781910197479

Naked I Stand is a must-read for all those on a healing pilgrimage. This is Christine's most intimate book to date. She writes intuitively and with raw honesty about the sensitive topics of sexual brokenness, domestic violence, co-dependency and emotional autism – much of it based on personal experience – as well as healing and breakthrough.

There is light at the end of the tunnel and it's not the train coming the other way! We all have broken areas in our lives and, if we are honest, God is waiting to pour Himself into our wounds. We are deeply loved even in our struggle.

If you need a book with answers and breakthrough ministry, this is for you.

"Get this book in your life!" – Rev. Ray Scorey
Dir. Norwich Healing Rooms, UK

Available from all good bookshops and the publisher:
www.onwardsandupwards.org